GIVEN TO:

_____

BY:

_____

DATE:

_____

*To: Sherry*

# FINDING YOUR GLASSES:

## Revealing and Achieving Authentic Success

*Inspire the world with your AOTuns*

*James 22*

Uncover the 6 Basic Lenses of Success to
Pursue your Purpose, Passion, and Priorities

# Justin Jones-Fosu, MBA

Author of Inspiration for Life: Dream Bigger, Do More, Live Fuller

Finding Your Glasses
Revealing and Achieving Authentic Success

ISBN: 978-0-9833718-0-9

Published by Peter Jones Publishing
Post Office Box 72122
Baltimore, Maryland 21237

Available from:

www.justininspires.com

www.findingyourglasses.com

This book is dedicated to the following:

**My mother (Mom-e)**
Thank you for raising me with priorities in mind. All of your glasses lying around the house were an inspiration to me. I think I found several of your lost glasses throughout the years.

**The Memory of Danielle Rice**
She will always be remembered for her love for life and her win-win mindset. She inspired me to live life like every day counts, and for that I am forever grateful!

**You**
Thank you for desiring authentic success. I pray you find it through your journey.

# CONTENTS

## PART I: A FIRST LOOK

## PART II: THE 6 BASIC LENSES OF SUCCESS

# PART III: VISION ADJUSTMENT

# FOREWORD

I ate my meals in the dining hall, as most college freshmen did. I remember looking forward to dinner because I would be able to spend time with my friends. This group of friends, later deemed the "Freshmen Fam," was a unique bunch. Dinner conversations were laced with deep thoughts concerning life, love, education, and politics. We would sit for hours debating and sharing ideas. It was there that I met Justin Jones-Fosu.

While in college, Justin was Mr. Morgan State University, President of the Marketing Society and School of Business Student Leadership Council. With his natural ability leadership and tenacity to motivate, it makes sense that Justin would write a book to inspire change in the lives of people.

In *Finding Your Glasses: Revealing and Achieving Authentic Success*, Justin questions: *"Why let society, the media, or others define what success looks like to you when you can find and achieve your own prescription on life?"* He then offers tools to begin answering this question. This book provides a practical process on how to create and live an authentically successful life.

At some point, everyone falls prey to the all-encompassing idea of what you are "supposed to do". I was supposed to go to college, go to graduate school, and buy a home. I did all of those things, but still felt unsuccessful. The reality is that it is a lot easier living life by norms, and the "supposed to do's." The harder task is accessing whether you are happy or not. If you are not content, are you willing to venture off the path of complacency to find that happiness?

You've already taken the first step by picking up this book. Start creating your own personalized plan for a better career, better relationships, and ultimately a better life! Enjoy!!!

- **Sophia Franklin, Biggest Loser Contestant Season 10**

# INTRODUCTION

Have you ever put on someone else's glasses? How did your eyes feel? You probably felt the same way I did when I tried on my mom's reading glasses as a child. Her glasses were very strong, but I wanted to see if I could withstand her potent prescription. I put them on with confidence but was forced to immediately take them off with discomfort, after slowly shedding a tear or two. The tears did not fall because I was sad, but rather because her prescription really hurt my eyes.

So you may be asking – what does this have to do with success? Everything! As I have been traveling the country consulting and speaking with thousands of professionals, students and various other populations about *Unleashing their Visions*, I realized that people were not really unleashing their own visions, but rather visions that had been given to them by the media, their parents, or by many books written on "success". People's eyes (vision) have been hurting. I became curious as to why so many individuals were "wearing" other people's glasses by trying to achieve visions that were not unique to them. I would hear various stories; challenges of balancing work and life, stories of wanting to live comfortably, stories of wanting to do more; but never actually acting. Throughout this book you will discover why you no longer have to live by these reasons, or any other reasons that might currently exist in your life.

## This Book Is For You If...

1. You are chasing after the popular view of success (money, power, possessions, and fame) while forsaking your core values.

2. You are not trying to pursue your dreams, vision, and goals, but have settled for a life that is less than your hopes and dreams.

3. You are on the journey of authentic success and you want to achieve more for yourself, your family, your community, and the world at large.

## No Easy Authentic Success

Let me be very clear - I am neither for nor against nor money, power, possessions, and fame. In fact, I know many who have all of these things and are on their journey of authentic success. Nevertheless, I also know many who have these things and are not happy. In this book you will be challenged to confront the real you. You will determine if there is true alignment between your core values and your actions. This determination, for many, is an eye opening experience.

If you are looking for a book on how to be an overnight success in five steps, or how to accomplish your dreams by paying only $99.99 in five installments, then this book will not answer your questions or give you what you desire. To be quite honest, I am disgusted at the books, the methods, and infomercials that try to make "success" seem as easy as possible to attain! If you are looking for a short-term book that is nothing more than a mere fad, then this book is not for you.

However, if you are looking for a guide, to help you achieve authentic success that is uniquely designed and prescribed for you, then you have the right book. If you are looking for a tool that you can use to learn and grow from years later, then this book will help you accomplish those goals. By reading this book you will gain a deeper understanding of what you REALLY want in life and what matters the most to you. You will also be inspired by over 30 real stories of others who are now on the journey of authentic success. You will learn how to be more effective, to create and achieve more directed goals, and create a plan for your family, career, and community with the Clarifying Cycle of Success Model ™.

On this journey, the 6 Basic Lenses of Success™ will be instrumental to creating and living an authentically successful life. They were created to give you a simple and practical process to apply action to your core values.

Lens 1: Reflective Thinking (Where Have I Been)
Lens 2: Empowering Vision (Where Am I Going)
Lens 3: Targeted Planning (How Will I Get There)
Lens 4: Inspiring ACTion (What Will I do)
Lens 5: Nagging Persistence (How Will I Overcome)
Lens 6: Appreciative Celebration How Will I Celebrate)

## How to R.E.A.D. This Book:

1. **R**ead each chapter for comprehension and not just to complete it. I have noticed that many now read books to share how many books they have read, or just to know the latest concept or model. Few actually read to gain as much as they can and allow the principles to change their attitude, perspective, actions, and overall life. Completely understand the Clarifying Cycle of Success Model, which is made up of the 6 Basic Lenses of Success, as you will be able to use this in all areas of your life.

2. **E**ngage in the material and exercises throughout the book, as they are designed to help you uncover more about yourself and how you will move forward with success.

Highlight and underline words, stories, or anything that has meaning for you. Come back to it periodically to make sure that you remain on the journey of moving forward with authentic success. The more you engage with the material the easier applying and ACTing upon it will come.

3. **A**pply and ACT on the principles shared throughout this book. It is not enough to simply read and engage with the material, if you never actually apply what you learn. The end of each chapter contains both a summary and an "ACTion items" section. This section is designed to help you ACT on what you have read.

4. **D**iscuss what you have learned from each chapter with a friend, a family member, or anyone that you choose to. It is proven that if you can teach and share what you have learned then it actually enhances your ability to comprehend and apply what you have learned. Challenge yourself at the end of every chapter to not move on until you have shared what you have learned and what you will do.

What I will share with you in this book is not rocket science, or some exclusive code for only those who can see life a certain way. It is a simple and practical process to have success on the terms that you decide. Even though the model is practical and simple, the process will be challenging because societies definition of success is so engrained in human culture. The information I will share with you is based on my experience, extensive research, and countless hours of formal and informal conversations and interviews. Let's get ready to begin this exciting and fulfilling journey of authentic success! Let's find your glasses!

# CHAPTER ONE
# 20/20 VISION-A NEW LOOK AT SUCCESS

"Success is liking yourself, liking what you do, and liking how you do It." – Maya Angelou

*" The journey of Erin the eagle "*

As we begin, let me tell you a story about Erin the eagle. You will probably be able to relate to this eagle, if not right away, surely by the end of the book. Erin is like us all in that she desires to live a life full of happiness, success, and joy.

### *The Journey Begins*

Erin was an eagle who lived most of her life in the deep woods. Erin woke up every day with adventure on her heart – desiring to accomplish great things in life.

One day, after a very adventurous time soaring in the sky, Erin grew more tired than normal. She fluffed her feathers and nestled into the bosom of her wing. A deep sleep soon overtook her, and she experienced a rather peculiar dream. In the dream, while soaring, Erin could not see clearly and continually heard a faint voice whispering "you will need glasses if you want to see me." She flew higher and higher, and the voice became louder and louder until it rang out like thunder. She then woke abruptly realizing it was the early dawn of morning, but there was one problem: she could no longer see clearly. Erin was fearful of what had just occurred and did not know how she would find food for the day.

She immediately flew out of her nest on the journey to find her glasses. She stopped by the first animal she could recognize, who happened to be Rob the Rabbit. Erin asked Rob, "Do you know where my glasses are?" Rob quickly replied that he had not seen her glasses, but insisted that if she wore a pair of his glasses she would be faster than ever on her journey. Erin was little confused by his response, but she put on Rob's glasses and continued on her quest to find her glasses. Erin noticed that she was soaring faster than normal, but she still could see clearly. Erin was a little frustrated and not content with Rob the Rabbit's glasses.

She then flew to Sylvester the Snake. She did not get too close to him because she heard he was a very sneaky creature that would say anything to get his way. She cautiously asked Sylvester, "Do you know where my glasses are?" and Sylvester slickly replied, "try my glasses on and you can persuade the other animals to do what you want them to." Erin thought this response was bizarre but she put on Sylvester the Snake's glasses anyway. She noticed that she could persuade the other animals, but she still could not see clearly nor was she content with Sylvester the Snake's glasses.

Erin, growing extremely hungry and weary of her travel, searched for Olivia the Owl. Olivia was known for her great wisdom. When Erin finally found Olivia, she asked, "Do you know where my glasses are?" Olivia gave great wisdom and said very clearly, "When the sun initially touches the water you will find your glasses." Olivia then gave Erin a pair of her glasses to wear.

Erin felt wiser than normal, but she still could not see clearly. She was not content with Olivia the Owl's glasses.

At this point, Erin was both tired and frustrated. She developed a headache from wearing three different pair of glasses. She found a lake and decided to rest. Erin was extremely discontent as she glanced into the clear water of the lake. To her surprise, she saw an animal in the water…

To be continued…

 *An interview that changed my life.*

Several years ago, I was a brand-marketing intern with an international beverage company. The company invited 49 diverse students from across the country to be a part of this inaugural program; it was simply an honor to participate. They paid for us to live in a hotel the entire summer, paid us $5,000.00 for 10 weeks (and as a 20 year old that was a lot of money), and gave us a $10,000.00 scholarship each summer. Can you see why I liked it so much?

While there, I worked on the launch of one of their new drinks, a branding initiative for one of their older brands, and I had the opportunity to share the leadership in a million dollar marketing campaign. While all these opportunities were great, there was one special opportunity that changed my life forever. I had the opportunity to separately interview three senior level executives for the company. I did not want to ask them regular questions. I wanted to stand out in a positive way so I asked one simple question, "If you had to do everything exactly as you did it, would you do it again?"

Each of the executives seemed a little shocked by my question, but appeared to answer honestly. The first executive responded "no"; "I would have spent more time with my family." The second executive also replied no, and shared that he would have pursued his hobby. The third said he would have done everything exactly the same.

If you are anything like me you are surprised by the answers of the first two executives. All three of these senior level executives were grossing well over $200,000.00 a year, had access to the company helicopter and yacht, and could go to the major league baseball games and sit right behind home plate in the company's luxurious suite. Yet, two out of the three would have changed the course of their careers, while putting more emphasis on their core values.

This opportunity changed my life. I walked out of those interviews certain that I did not want to wake up later in life and realize that I was not living my passion, my dreams, and not valuing what matters most to me. I did not want to live a life full of should haves, could haves, and overwhelming regret. What about you?

## SOCIETAL SUCCESS DEFINED

Webster's online dictionary defines success as follows:
1. A degree or measure of succeeding
2. A favorable desire or outcome; also: the attainment of wealth, favor, or eminence

Now while I agree with the first definition and the first clause of the second, it was not surprising to me that money and power were included in the definition of success. Unfortunately, I have come to believe that money, power, possessions, and fame are what most people relate to when they think of success. That is what I call societal success.

## REFLECTION EXERCISE 1.1

Are you successful? If so, why do you think you are successful? If not, why don't you think you are successful? How do you ultimately define success? Take a moment to write out your honest answers to these questions.

_____

_____

_____

_____

_____

_____

_____

_____

_____

_____

_____

_____

_____

_____

_____

_____

_____

_____

_____

_____

_____

In *Achieving Authentic Success,* Ron Jenson mentions the five P's of how society normally defines success:

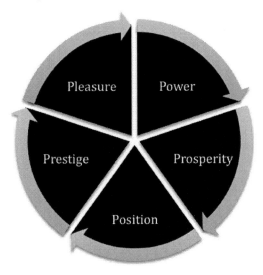

A paradigm is defined as a typical example or a philosophical mindset. The five P's are a paradigm that exists for success and it is a powerful influence on most people. The way people define success is definitely a mindset, because if you watch late night television you will see countless infomercials promising effortless success if you buy their product or DVD. You will also see many books throughout bookstores on achieving societal success by implementing this once in a lifetime method (sarcasm intended).

People come up to me after my presentations and constantly state their displeasure with where they currently are in life. So many people feel they are stuck in lifestyles built upon a life they never wanted to live. The sad truth is that I am certain there are many more who feel the same way, that never came up to me after my presentations.

---

**REFLECTION EXERCISE 1.2**

Take a moment to rate the enjoyment of your current life from 1
to 5 (with 1 being "do not enjoy" and 5 being "absolutely enjoy").
Why did you rate yourself this way?

_____

_____

_____

_____

_____

_____

---

You may be wondering what is so bad about societal success.
Nothing is wrong with it as long as that idea of success does not
overtake your core values in life (which you will uncover in
Chapter 2). There are many dangers associated with just pursuing
societal success:

1. Living a life without close, intimate, and loving
   relationships
2. A never ending journey to always acquire more, which
   leads to decreased happiness
3. Lack of confidence in who you are, with relying on
   confidence built on what you have

With so many dangers why do people wear the glasses of societal
success and others? People wear the glasses of the following:

1. Parents
2. Family/Relatives
3. Celebrities/Icons
4. Friends

5. Media and Advertising
6. Co-workers

Through personal experience and many of the interviews I have conducted, it is evident that people wear another's glasses to impress others, or to compensate for low self-esteem. This was my experience for many years. I desired to go to one of the top schools because it would make my dad proud (he is a Northwestern alumnus). When I had low self-esteem I would do anything to make him or others proud, because through their approval I found my identity. I always knew that he wanted the best for me, however he was giving me what he felt was best for him and trying to make that fit me. There is nothing wrong with attending the top schools, but one must determine if what is being offered is the right fit for what is desired from an educational experience. The danger we face is that people are becoming copies and losing their originality. I had to be careful not to be "just like" my dad. The danger we face is that people are becoming copies and losing their originality. Neglecting to tailor our own personal and professional experiences to desired dreams and goals becomes a serious detriment to our unique visions.

## THE COPY FACTOR

The copy factor takes place when others try to be just like someone else in dress, style, speech, or any other area. While growing up I tried to be just like Michael Jackson. I went to school with my white sparkling glove, my black penny loafers, white socks, and high-water pants. I was "BAD" and I knew it! As I matured I grew to appreciate myself. Even though I sometimes still do some of his moves I have learned to find and create my own! One of my most popular sayings is *"Why be just like anyone, when you can be better than everyone, by being the only you!"*

I like what Oscar Wilde conveys when he says, "Most people are other people. Their thoughts are someone else's opinions, their lives a mimicry, their passions a quotation." Do you know people like this? You see them on college campuses as ladies and guys that are trying to be just like a group of people; and some allow their identity to be formed by an organization or club that they join.

You see them in the professional ranks as the "yes people", those that always agree with the manager or executive, regardless of the situation. They find out what the manager likes and all of the sudden they miraculously like it too! In Simon Bailey's book, *Releasing Your Brilliance,* he calls these kinds of people cubic zirconiums. These people are only imitations of the real thing, and lack a sense of identity. They live out what appears to be success for someone else. These people are easy to spot, like the Jack Welch imitators, the movie star imitators, and especially the mass imitators of the "it" celebrities of today.

Let me be clear – there is nothing wrong with emulating the positive behaviors of others, if it is authentic to you, and/or it is something that lines up with your system of core values. What I have witnessed is that many individuals are not necessarily imitating other people, but rather promoting an outlook of success, and often this is merely a materialistic ideology.

## REFLECTION EXERCISE 1.3

Write out a time when have you tried to imitate another person or tried to fit into a certain perception. Why did you want to be like him or her? How did/do you feel about that time in your life?

## IS MATERIALISM REALLY BAD?

When I am asked this question, I respond by saying this: having things is not inherently bad, but it is a problem when things have us. What does this look like? It looks like a person that lives at home with his or her parents (not for medical or care reasons) but has an expensive luxury vehicle. It looks like a person living paycheck to paycheck but has all of the newest shoes and fashions. It looks like a person sacrificing his or her integrity and character in order to attain more material wealth and possessions.

According to a 2006 NY Times article, *"Materialism is Bad For You?"* studies show that there is growing evidence and research that the downsides of excessive getting and spending are damaging with the following:

1. Relationships and self-esteem
2. The Heightened risk of depression and anxiety
3. Less time with what the research says makes a person truly happy like family, friendship, and engaging work.

Materialism can go on and on, and for most it can be a never-ending journey. The bar of achievement continues to climb higher and higher. When some finally reach it, he or she realizes it was not worth what he or she sacrificed to get there.

A recent survey shows that in the last few years Americans' priorities with an emphasis on wealth, financial stability, money, professional attainment, and success have nearly doubled to 17%. Two of the areas in the study that dropped were family and faith, which are still the top priorities, according to the study. I believe this increase speaks not only to the economic challenges many Americans are facing, but also the continual focus on wealth and money as a priority.

Ed Diener, a University of Illinois psychology professor and happiness expert states, "Those who value material success more than they value happiness are likely to experience almost as many negative moods as positive moods, whereas those who value happiness over material success are likely to experience considerably more pleasant moods and emotions than unpleasant moods and emotions."

**REFLECTION EXERCISE 1.4**
Write down what living the American Dream means to you. After you write it down check to see if it matches the quote by James Truslow Adams. Do you see any major differences or similarities in what you wrote versus what Adams shared on the next page?

Well you may ask isn't the great American Dream directly related to materialism? For many there is a direct link between material success and the American Dream. I believe that the American "Dream" has turned into the American Nightmare with the ever-increasing and insatiable desire of more "stuff." James Truslow Adams, who coined the phrase "American Dream" stated in his 1931 book *Epic in America,*

> The American Dream that has lured tens of millions of all nations to our shores in the past century has not been a dream of material plenty, though that has doubtlessly counted heavily. It has been a dream of being able to grow to fullest development as a man and woman, unhampered by the barriers which had slowly been erected in the older civilizations, unrepressed by social orders which had developed for the benefit of classes rather than for the simple human being of any and every class.

The true question here is what do we consider our "fullest development"? Is it the luxury car, the mansion, and 2.5 children, or is it something deeper, something of more value, something of great substance that feeds our inner happiness?

## DEFINING AUTHENTIC SUCCESS

*"Authentic success is knowing that if you left the world today, you'd leave with no regrets"* - Unknown

According to Webster's online dictionary being "authentic is being true to one's own personality, spirit, and character." Authentic success is when individuals or organizations actions align with their core values. It begins internally and then it impacts the external, whereas societal success starts off externally and usually ends the same way – externally. This is seen true with the differences between extrinsic (external) versus intrinsic (internal) motivations. In *True North* Bill George uses the following table to further define the two.

| Extrinsic Motivations | Intrinsic Motivations |
|---|---|
| ♦ Monetary compensation<br>♦ Having power<br>♦ Having a title<br>♦ Public recognition<br>♦ Social status<br>♦ Winning over others | ♦ Personal Growth<br>♦ Satisfaction of doing a good job<br>♦ Helping others develop<br>♦ Finding meaning from efforts<br>♦ Being true to one's belief<br>♦ Making a difference in the world |

### REFLECTION EXERCISE 1.5

Take a moment to put a check next to the items that you have been concerned with over the last year? Are you surprised by what you see? Why or why not?

_____
_____
_____
_____
_____
_____
_____
_____
_____
_____
_____

While authentic success is birthed out of intrinsic motivations, it does not mean that you will never receive extrinsic rewards. All it means is your desire is birthed from within. I realized this when I was selected as one of EBONY magazines "Top 30 Young Leaders on the Rise." I never sought out the award, but what I sought after was making a difference in my community, building a business around my strength and passions, and making a difference in the everyday lives of those around me. INROADS, an intern organization with which I was formerly an intern, reached out to me and let me know it was nominating me.

Honestly, I was humbled that EBONY would even think of me. They emailed me and let me know I made it through the first round of selections, and I was humbled that I made it that far. EBONY called me next and asked when I could do a photo shoot because I made it to the final round of selection. Next thing I know I am in the February 2008 edition of EBONY Magazine, and I still was just humbled that people would care enough to see me living my passions, dreams, and adding value to my community and others would recognize me for it.

I never sought after this award, but my intrinsic motivations produced an extrinsic reward. To this day I have people ask me what they need to do to receive this award or other awards that I have received, and most seem shocked by my consistent response. Many who ask me want the prestige of it, the public recognition, or the title. But I share with them to follow their passions, driven by their core values, and make a difference in society. I encourage you to do the same whether you want this or any award!

Whether with awards or not, authentic success is a journey not a destination. You are either on the journey of authentic success or you are not. This journey is all about progression not perfection, because it is very rare that one ever reaches a place where 100% of their actions line up with their core values. I have not reached that place, and the over 30 people I interviewed also have not, but they are consciously working toward it every day.

## REAL LIFE AUTHENTIC SUCCESS

*"Dream as if you'll live forever, live as if you'll die today!"* – James Dean

Authentic success challenges you to sacrifice what is least important for what is most important. If you are sacrificing your primary core values, then it is not authentic success. There are usually two extremes when people think about success. One extreme is what we have already discussed as societal success, where all that matters is achieving more money, more power, more possessions, and more fame. The other extreme is where people are essentially just getting by, and refuse to receive any extrinsic rewards. They feel their success is built on not having anything of extrinsic value. This can also be called false humility. Authentic success is in the middle of these two extremes. Our society produces many examples of authentic success if we would just stop and look around us.

 ***Scott Harrison: Water can change a life.***
In 2004 Scott Harrison made a decision that would alter his life forever. Before that he was a very "successful" nightclub and fashion event promoter. He was rubbing shoulders and living the high life with the Who's Who of the Big Apple. For the most part he was living very selfishly and arrogantly, but he desperately

wanted something more. Scott was unhappy and felt the need to reconnect with his Christian faith as he faced what he stated was "spiritual bankruptcy." He asked a simple question.

*"What would the opposite of my life look like?"*

He signed up for volunteer service aboard a floating hospital with a group called Mercy Ships. This humanitarian organization offered free medical care to the world's poorest nations. Top doctors and surgeons left their comfortable lives to operate for free on thousands who had no access to medical care. This was definitely a transition for Scott, as he became the ship's photojournalist.

I traded my spacious midtown loft for a 150-square-foot cabin with bunk beds, roommates, and cockroaches. Fancy restaurants were replaced by a mess hall feeding 400+ Army style. A prince in New York, now I was living in close community with 350 others. I felt like a pauper. But once off the ship, I realized how good I really had it. In new surroundings, I was utterly astonished at the poverty that came into focus through my camera lens. Often through tears, I documented life and human suffering I'd thought unimaginable. In West Africa, I was a prince again. A king, in fact. A man with a bed and clean running water and food in my stomach.

After some time with this group, Scott traveled back to New York with a newfound passion, and a sense of urgency to make a difference. With his understanding that billions of people needed access to clean water, he invited 700 of his friends to his 31st birthday party and encouraged each to bring $20 in order raise funds for a clean water project in Uganda. The life-changing organization *charity: water* was born. It did not stop there, because the next year he asked people to donate $32 for his 32nd birthday and he asked others to join him in giving up their birthdays. In that one initiative they raised over $150,000 for hospitals and schools in Kenya.

The organization has now raised more than 10 million dollars and helped over one million people. What impressed me about our interview was that Scott was not satisfied with what had been done, but rather he still sees the great need to provide clean water for those in need. Scott is definitely on his journey of authentic success as his actions are in alignment with his core values.

### *Juanita Rogers: Family is a Priority.*

When Juanita Rogers was at the world-renowned Johns Hopkins University as a Pre-Med student she was on top of the world. She knew that her desire of being a doctor would likely be fulfilled. Juanita got married, had a child, and struggled with the decision to apply to Medical School.

When Juanita was 12 her father left, and her remaining family moved to Texas. She grew up seeing her mother as the stabilizer in times of transition. She had to make a decision whether to stay at home or go to medical school. After careful reflection she decide to be a full-time housewife; as her children grew older she became a home-school mother.

While she admits that not everyone's path will be like hers or should be like hers, she is very adamant that you cannot forsake your values for desires of great notoriety.

I am thankful for the things that I have like a home and a family. I have the ability to see the lessons taking root in my children, and I get to see their growth and development. To see my children's milestones means a lot. In shifting to authentic success the biggest thing is patience! You should not drag your feet, but you must understand that there is a process.

There are also many who are not on the journey of authentic success. These are the kinds of people that tell themselves that they wish they could have spent more quality time with the people they love, but yet they still seek after societal success with no regard to their core values. Years of their lives have passed with no changes. This can be seen no matter if a person was born to "successful" people or not. In *Crush It* by Gary Vaynerchuk, he shares that there are a lot of ambitious people that have great DNA, but are at a professional standstill, frustrated, miserable and stuck. He shares that they are this way because they were not doing what they loved more than anything in the world. They were not doing what they were born to do.

For some reason we have created this mental model that we cannot have both a great career and a great family life, or a great career and a great personal life. The over-indulgence of the career is what does not allow us to have all of the above. You can still do well in your career and have a great family and personal life. I am a current example of that now, and many of those interviewed are examples as well. One thing almost all of us had to do was change!

## THE CHALLENGES OF CHANGE

*"There is nothing wrong with change, if it is in the right direction."*
– Winston Churchill

There are great risks in traveling the journey of authentic success. Some other risks will be addressed in Chapter 11, but the biggest risks that I see are never beginning at all or never getting back on the journey of authentic success. People are literally risking their happiness and enjoyment everyday. In *The Now Habit*, Neil Fiore shares the reluctance of leaving the familiar for the unfamiliar, and that we are reluctant because we must undergo the awkward first steps of the beginner.

I know this feeling all too well. I worked for a major retailer as one of their store managers. Even as a new leader I was already on tours to other stores with the district manager, giving my opinion to some who had been in the position for years. I was also leading a team of over 50 people, but I soon discovered a passion for training.

At the age of 26 I left to become a Training Coordinator for a major financial services firm in Baltimore. I was now the low person on the totem pole and no longer had a team to lead. Instead, I was supporting everyone else. It was awkward, stressful, and there were many moments when I wanted to throw in the towel. That change, however, was one of the best decisions that I ever made. It gave me the foundation and experience that is proving to be a major competitive advantage for my own company.

I know some of you are saying, "but you were only 26 and it's easy to do that when you are young and early in your career." Let me share with you the story of my friend Tina, who unlike me had an established career.

### Tina M.: From Information Technology to Training

Tina started out working for the federal government in Personnel. She started right around the time when Information Technology

(IT) was gaining momentum in the workplace. Tina said, "*When you are young, you are looking at how you can make the most money,*" and that's just what she did. In her department she became the go-to person for IT matters. After she spent more than 26 years, she became a little frustrated. She noticed that in IT there was more of a focus on the operational and technical side and less focus on the people. You see people were Tina's real passion.

Since she was an IT manager, Tina was afforded the opportunity to have a coach. Through the coach's assistance she went through a period of reflection and realized that her dream job was to lead a training organization. She saw an opening, but realized that one of the requirements was a Masters degree. Instead of staying where she was, she took action and applied to an HR Masters program.

She also overcame the challenges of change by doing all she could to gain the HR/Personnel experience within her department. Any time there was an opportunity to train the other members, Tina volunteered. She knew that when changing careers you sometimes have to start at the bottom, but she also said this:

> It would be easy to stay where I am, and not make any changes, but my passion for learning and development won't let me do that.

Tina's passion was not IT. She knew it would require a lot of courage for anyone to follow their passion after being in one field for so many years. She knew there was the great potential for less pay, but with courage she forged ahead.

I have seen people for more than 20 years who come to work for 8 hours everyday and look at the clock all day to signal when they can go home. They do not enjoy what they do. It is merely a job to them. Hopefully, people will come to the point and take the risk and make the change toward following their passion!

Tina took that risk. She knew that other departments and organizations would want both experience and education. She did not allow that to be a reason why she could not follow her passion. She was willing to make the sacrifices for her journey of authentic success. Are you willing to do the same?

**REFLECTION EXERCISE 1.6**

Have you ever wanted to switch careers, or start your own business, or be a stay at home parent and never did it? What stopped you? What were the factors that minimized your personal change effort? Write down your responses.

_____

_____

_____

_____

_____

_____

_____

_____

_____

_____

_____

_____

In *Success Intelligence*, Robert Holden states, "(T)he highest truth about success and sacrifice is that success requires you to sacrifice what is not important for what is. If your idea of success leads you to sacrifice what you most value, surely it is not true success."

I believe that many people do not pursue change for many reasons. Here are some of the statements that I have heard:

*"I cannot change what I am doing, because I need to make the money necessary to support the lifestyle that my family is living."*

*"It will be too hard to do that at this age. All I want to do is retire and collect my pension."*

*"I am just a few promotions away from the top position, maybe I will love that position."*

*"Losing the weight just seems too hard to do. Plus I can't miss my favorite TV shows to do it"*

*"I am just not comfortable with the risk, what if I fail, and what if things don't go the way I want them to go. It really is just too much of a risk for me."*

*"My parents want me to major in this field, and I don't want to upset them. I think I can deal with it for a couple more years, even if I don't like it."*

One of the central themes that I have discovered is the simple fact that we have been conditioned to seek a certain life, go to a certain kind of school, get a certain kind of job, make a certain amount of money, have a certain kind of spouse, have a certain kind of house, have certain kinds of friends, have certain kinds of children, go on certain kinds of vacations, retire a certain kind of way, and then we die.

What if I told you that much of this is all a marketing ploy? What if the media have been so smart that they have tapped into shaping our wants and desires so well that now we believe we actually need it all. Think about it! There are credit card commercials that insinuate if you pay with cash you are messing up the happy flow of people (research shows that people pay 14-16% more when they pay with credit card versus cash). There are car commercials that say, "Who wouldn't want a bigger and better car?"

I majored in Marketing; for many years I participated in this kind of influencing. I personally do not believe that there is anything wrong with marketing. I do not think there is anything wrong with a majority of the commercials that exist, but I do think it is wrong when we sacrifice what is most important for what we are marketed. It is wrong when we say that we want a great family, but we work 60-80 hours a week and we never see our family. It is wrong when we say I care about my faith or giving back to the community, but yet our actions never seem to align with what we are saying.

If we do not grasp this central concept that we must lead with our core values and follow consistently with our actions, we will forge along in life never actualizing authentic success. For many it will remain a far away land that is nice to think about, but we would never dare try to reach. Some may even try behavior modification, but that will not have a long-term impact without a changed mindset. If you take this journey seriously and do not close your mind to the possibility of something more, then the rest of the book will help you to get one step closer.

Let me ease your concerns. You do not have to accomplish everything overnight, but the only thing I would encourage you to do is to let down your barriers to what you and I have been conditioned to believe, and for some of us it has gone unnoticed. Why do so many of us live in debt and surprisingly no matter the income level still live paycheck to paycheck? Don't let this book be something you just read for the knowledge. Let the concepts, stories, and the practical process change your life. In the next chapter you will receive an "I" exam and uncover your core values to get back to 20/20 vision. You will definitely learn more about yourself. Enjoy the rest of your journey!

---

## ✔ ACTION ITEMS:

---

1. Over the last year what have you sacrificed? Have you sacrificed what is most important to you or what is not most important to you?
2. In order to be more authentically successful what do you need to Start, Stop, and Continue doing?
3. Write down what stood out the most to you from this chapter, and why it stood out to you.
4. What is one thing that you will do or think differently because of reading this chapter?
5. Don't forget to share with someone else within 24 hours what you have learned. If you can, try to do it before you move on to the next chapter.

Visit www.findingyourglasses.com for more resources, exercises, tips, and tools on gaining a new look on success.

## CHAPTER TWO:
# THE "I" EXAM: THE MIRROR OF INTROSPECTION

*"Try not to become a man of success, but rather try to become a man of value"*
– Albert Einstein

## *"Two Cars on a Highway"*

There are two cars on the highway. Both are driving side-by-side and heading toward the same destination. One car is the new Mercedes Benz S-Class. It is equipped with all of the amenities a person could ever want in a car: a built-in GPS, dual heating/cooling system, and a sunroof. It has a sleek silver exterior with chrome rims for the wheels. This car is truly a head turner.

The other car is a 1984 Oldsmobile with all the "amenities" that you would never want in a car. The heat and air conditioning systems do not work. The radio does not work. The windows are manual, and only two of the windows roll down. The exterior is even worse; it is all rusty. The paint is chipping off. It has missing hubcaps and scratches all over.

Which one of these cars would you say is more successful? When I ask this question during my presentations, it is interesting to see how people respond. Most people raise their hands for the Mercedes Benz as the obvious choice because of its great beauty and functionality. Others raise their hands for the 1984 Oldsmobile because they either like old cars, or they believe I am trying to trick them with all my challenges to the normal paradigms of success. There are many others who do not raise their hands at all for fear of being wrong. Which car do you think is more successful?

The answer is neither. We cannot tell which one is more successful. Just because the Mercedes is new and looks great on the outside does not mean that it is more successful. Just because the Oldsmobile is a classic does not mean that it is more successful. The correct question is this: *What is on the inside?*

What really matters is how much gas each car has. It does not matter what the outside looks like if it runs out of gas and never reaches its intended destination. What is inside of us? What matters most is what is fueling us. That is what will help us reach our intended destination. Most of my participants' initial response to the question highlights the value on outward appearance.

## EXPECTATIONS FOR CHAPTER

Throughout this chapter you will have time to look at what is fueling you. You will be able to reflect and work through your core values, and strengths. I encourage you to be very honest with yourself and take a hard and long look in the mirror. I challenge you to not think of what the *right* answer is, but rather what is your authentic answer.

# THE AUTHENTIC SUCCESS ASSESSMENT (ASA)

Please circle the answer that most clearly defines where you are at this moment. If you are not a student, please fill out the questions relating to the career aspect of the question. If you are a student please fill out the "major" aspect of the question. We can only grow through self-awareness, so allow this assessment to take a snapshot of where you are as it relates to authentic success. Again, there are no right or wrong answers. Answer honestly! In the *What's Next Appendix* you will see that I encourage you to retake this assessment in 30 days and again six months to gauge your progress. You will also see instructions on how to make this a part of your annual check-up.

**Assessment Key:**
SD=Strongly Disagree (1)
Di=Disagree (2)
Ag=Agree (3)
SA-Strongly Agree (4)

|  | Question | SD (1) | Di (2) | Ag (3) | SA (4) |
|---|---|---|---|---|---|
| 1 | I am happy with my life. | 1 | 2 | 3 | 4 |
| 2 | I could die today without any regrets. | 1 | 2 | 3 | 4 |
| 3 | My life has meaning. | 1 | 2 | 3 | 4 |

# The "I" Exam

| | Question | SD (1) | Di (2) | Ag (3) | SA (4) |
|---|---|---|---|---|---|
| 4 | I am completely satisfied with my life. | 1 | 2 | 3 | 4 |
| 5 | I am likely to accomplish my goals. | 1 | 2 | 3 | 4 |
| 6 | I am guided in life by a clear vision statement. | 1 | 2 | 3 | 4 |
| 7 | I plan my time/day everyday. | 1 | 2 | 3 | 4 |
| 8 | I create and follow goals that positively challenge me. | 1 | 2 | 3 | 4 |
| 9 | I have friends with whom I am honest/transparent. | 1 | 2 | 3 | 4 |
| 10 | I am more likely to be myself, rather than to be what others expect me to be. | 1 | 2 | 3 | 4 |
| 11 | I define success more by who I am, rather than what I have. | 1 | 2 | 3 | 4 |
| 12 | What others think of me does not affect how I feel about myself. | 1 | 2 | 3 | 4 |
| 13 | I am happy (at work/with my major). | 1 | 2 | 3 | 4 |
| 14 | My (career/major) is fulfilling and rewarding. | 1 | 2 | 3 | 4 |

| | Question | SD (1) | Di (2) | Ag (3) | SA (4) |
|---|---|---|---|---|---|
| 15 | I love my (career/major). | 1 | 2 | 3 | 4 |
| 16 | I have an established set of values/beliefs. | 1 | 2 | 3 | 4 |
| 17 | I never compromise my beliefs for others. | 1 | 2 | 3 | 4 |
| 18 | My daily actions align with what I feel are the most important people/things in my life. | 1 | 2 | 3 | 4 |
| 19 | I take full responsibility for the current state of my life. | 1 | 2 | 3 | 4 |
| 20 | I follow through on what I say I will do. | 1 | 2 | 3 | 4 |
| 21 | I am likely to overcome obstacles. | 1 | 2 | 3 | 4 |
| 22 | I make a positive difference in the lives of others. | 1 | 2 | 3 | 4 |
| 23 | I treat others as I would like to be treated. | 1 | 2 | 3 | 4 |
| 24 | I have positive and healthy relationships. | 1 | 2 | 3 | 4 |
| 25 | I am more likely to have a positive attitude instead of a negative one. | 1 | 2 | 3 | 4 |

| | Question | SD (1) | Di (2) | Ag (3) | SA (4) |
|---|---|---|---|---|---|
| 26 | My past experiences have made me a better person. | 1 | 2 | 3 | 4 |
| 27 | I am an optimist. | 1 | 2 | 3 | 4 |
| 28 | I spend time reflecting on my life monthly. | 1 | 2 | 3 | 4 |
| 29 | Every night before I go to bed I think about how I lived that day. | 1 | 2 | 3 | 4 |
| 30 | On a quarterly basis, I ask for feedback from my closest relationships on how I can improve. | 1 | 2 | 3 | 4 |
| **Column Sub-Totals** (Add up the numbers in each column) | | | | | |
| **Overall Total Score** (Add up all the column sub-totals) | | | | | |

Your Overall Total Score will be anywhere between 30 and 120.

The ASA evaluates the following nine factors of authentic success:

1. Authenticity and Transparency (4 questions).
2. Personal/Life Happiness (4 questions).
3. Planning and Vision/Goal Achievement (3 questions).
4. Career Satisfaction (3 questions).
5. Defined Values/Belief Systems (3 questions).
6. Proactive Personal Action (3 questions).
7. Positive Attitude (3 questions).
8. Healthy Relationships (3 questions).
9. Personal Reflection (3 questions).

Please see the following results ratings based on your score:

| 111-120 | You should be on the road speaking with me! You are a great example of mastering the journey of authentic success. However, there is always more room to grow. Keep growing on this journey and be sure to help others! The rest of the book will help you to continue growing, but pay special attention to Ch. 12 |
|---|---|
| 101-110 | You are living an authentically successful life. Many areas in your life are in balance. Make sure you are taking the time out to celebrate the small moments and to help others on their journey! |
| 81-100 | You are on the journey of authentic success, but need to focus on a few more key areas in your life. What two things would you do differently? Create an action plan to improve in those areas. |
| 61-80 | At times you are on the journey of authentic success, and at times you are not. You may allow life's circumstances to affect how you feel and what you do. Determine what are the 3-4 responses that you can focus on and create an action plan of how to improve in those areas. |
| 30-60 | It does not appear that you are on the journey of authentic success. I have great news for you. You can start today! Make a conscious decision to let this be the lowest you will ever score on this assessment and in life! If you take this book seriously, you will see great improvement. It is not about where you are now that counts, but where you end up! |

## THE FRAME OF EXCUSES

I meet people all the time who have an excuse for why they cannot progress. I worked with a gentleman for a few years. Every time I share ways to grow with him, he has an excuse as to why he is operating in his current behavioral pattern.

The fact is that all of us make excuses. Even I do at times, but we must to move past those excuses in order to see the real problem. Yes, I am very aware that there are sometimes situations that we cannot control, but we can no longer allow for excuses to be the reason that we do not keep going forward.

---

 **REFLECTION EXERCISE 2.1**

What are the excuses that you have made for why you have not embarked on the journey of authentic success? Write them down so that they can be branded as excuses and you can move on to solutions.

_____

_____

_____

_____

_____

_____

_____

_____

_____

_____

_____

---

Once we stop looking through the Frame of Excuses we can take responsibility for our actions, no matter who or what is involved. Don't let excuses hold you back any longer. Do whatever it takes to break the Frame of Excuses.

## CORE VALUES

### Nathaniel Benjamin: A Fianceé and His Dream Job

Nathaniel was several months away from getting married to his fianceé, Angela. He sought my advice about a big decision that he faced. He had to choose between two job offers. The first opportunity was his dream job of being a traveling trainer. If he took this job he would have the great benefits of traveling to cities across the world and being a full-fledged trainer. The second opportunity would allow him to manage a team of others, but he would not be as closely linked to training. The decision seems like a no-brainer, right? Most people would do almost anything for their dream job, but Nathaniel is not like most people.

The first opportunity would have taken Nathaniel away from home often in the beginning of his new marriage, and it would have required Angela and him to relocate. Relocating was a big step as Angela just found a job that she really liked. He spent time in reflection and sought advice from some close friends. What he realized was that his core value of family was higher than his core value of career. Even though the first opportunity was Nathaniel's dream job, his dream wife was more important to him. This is what he had to say about it:

> My passion to have a great marriage and be there for my wife was stronger than my passion for my dream job. I may be able to do my dream job later on, but this is a once-in-a-lifetime opportunity to do marriage right the first time. I do my best to live by this quote: 'At any point in your life are you willing to give up what you have in order to achieve what you desire?'

I have seen many people damage their marriages for their careers, even though family was more important to them. Nathaniel treasured his life with his wife more than he treasured his dream job. He is a great example of allowing his core values to be a guide for his actions. I know that Angela and his future children will appreciate it.

Essentially, core values are the main areas in your life that you value. The following diagram is an example of core values, but is not an exhaustive list:

**Exhibit 2.1**

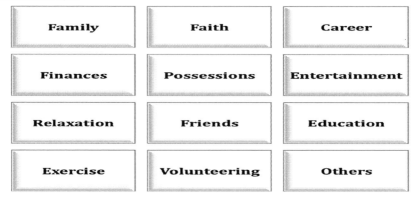

| Family | Faith | Career |
| Finances | Possessions | Entertainment |
| Relaxation | Friends | Education |
| Exercise | Volunteering | Others |

## PROFESSED, ESPOUSED, AND ENACTED VALUES

Professed values are values that are stated to others. Espoused values are values by which an individual prefers to live. Enacted values are values by which an individual actually lives. Many times these are three separate lists. For example, a person may profess a faith as a core value because he or she feels that is what is expected of them if they are running for a political office, but they may not live by it. An individual may say that volunteering is an important core value (professed and espoused), but have not volunteered for any causes in a year. Core values are your espoused values. Authentic success is when all three of the values are the same. When all of your core values line up, there is no difference from what you say, prefer, and do.

## CATEGORIES OF CORE VALUES

There are three categories of core values: *First Look, Second Look, and Third Look.*

**Exhibit 2.2**

|  | Explanation | What are yours? |
|---|---|---|
| **First Look Core Values (1-3)** | These core values are your top three and priority values. These are the most important areas in your life. Within your First Look Core Values is your primary core value (which is your #1 ranked core value). | 1. (Primary):<br><br>2.<br><br>3. |
| **Second Look Core Values (4-6)** | These core values are still very important to you, but rank lower than the First Look Core Values. | 4.<br><br>5.<br><br>6. |
| **Third Look Core Values (7 and beyond)** | These core values may still be important, but they are not as significant as the others. | 7.<br><br>8.<br><br>9.<br><br>10.<br><br>11. |

**🎆 REFLECTION EXERCISE 2.2**

If you could only pick one core value, which one would it be and why? Continue through the other core values and rank them based on the order of importance to YOU.

| Core Value | Ranking |
|---|---|
|  |  |
|  |  |
|  |  |
|  |  |
|  |  |
|  |  |
|  |  |
|  |  |
|  |  |

### Rafael Alvarez: My Family Time.

Rafael achieved a great deal. He was a high-performing employee for Compaq Computer Corporation (now HP) for over 11 years. He learned how to effectively handle the rigors of Corporate America and was doing very well.

Along his journey something touched him, and he saw an opportunity to make a difference. He decided to start a non-profit called Genesys Works. The organization provides economically disadvantaged high school students the knowledge and work experience required to succeed as professionals. Rafael worked long and hard to bring his dream to fruition. Although Rafael followed his heart with this worthwhile endeavor, there was something more important to him: his family.

I noticed that I was working many long hours for Genesys Works, but my family was suffering in the process. I decided to create a rule in my life. I would leave work at 5pm and I would be more present at home, because my family needed more of my time. Now there are still small exceptions to that rule if there are events after work, but I do all I can to be there for my family.

Rafael is still doing well with his organization and changing the lives of many young people, but he is also changing the lives of his family. He is an example that you can succeed at more than one core value.

While working on my MBA, I had to do a lot of group projects. On one project my group wanted to meet on Sunday at 11am. I attended church at the same time. Education is very important to me, but it is a Second Look Core Value, while faith is my First Look Core Value. I let my group know that I am free any time before 10am and after 2pm. For me this was a non-negotiable. I have other non-negotiables in my life, such as date night with my wife. Unless we agree to reschedule, our date night will not be moved.

## REFLECTION EXERCISE 2.3

What are the non-negotiables in your life? Write down your non-negotiables (which should be based on your core values) and share them with the people who matter in your life.

---

---

---

---

## THE REAL YOU

Who is the real you? Do you know you really are? I am not talking about the masks that we put up for our friends, family, and co-workers. I am also not talking about responses to people when we are at a networking event.

While in college I took a speech and communications class. The professor's name was Dr. Stephens. This was one of my favorite classes because I learned so much about myself. The last assignment for the class was a very unique one. First, she would have you sit in the middle of a circle while the rest of the class was on the outside. My classmates then went one by one and shared their impressions about me, both good and bad. All I could say was "thank you." Some of what they said made me feel really good, and other things not so good, but it was what people really thought.

The next phase of this project was to create a shoebox. On the outside of the shoebox I had to write what others thought of me, and in the inside of the shoebox I had to write what I thought about myself. (You can find my shoebox story on the www.findingyourglasses.com site.) I realized why I acted in certain ways. When I gave my speech to the class I was one of the many who broke out in tears because I tapped into the real me. I was beginning to really understand who I was.

That experience changed my life. To this day I have not forgotten it. What about you? Have you had an experience like this? When was the last time you really looked at the real you? Here are 5 ways to begin to uncover your true self:

1. **Become more self-aware**: Start being more conscious of what you do and do not do. If you hear something more

than once from a different person, you may want to pay attention.

> ### REFLECTION EXERCISE 2.4
> Write down who the *real* you is at the present moment. Then write down what you feel is the *best* you. What does your *best* self look like? What does your *best* self do? What does your *best* self think about?
>
> _____
> _____
> _____
> _____
> _____
> _____
> _____
> _____

2.  **Take personal assessments**: Here are some assessments that you can try: DISC Profile, Meyers Briggs, True Colors, Social Styles, and Career Anchors. Assessments like these and others will give you a better view of your true self. Understanding this is quite liberating

3.  **Spend some time by yourself:** Sometimes I learn so much about myself through personal times of reflection. I do my best to get away every once in a while in order to gain a better perspective of me.

4.  **Get coaching/counseling:** Too many people see counseling as a negative thing, but I believe in it in order to address things BEFORE they become issues, and even to deal with the current issues.

5. **Seek feedback from others:** Talk to people you trust and have your best interest in mind. Let them know you need them to tell you the truth about yourself. Then sit back, listen, and don't try to justify what they say. Like my shoebox activity, just say "thank you."

There are many other ways to get to know the real you. Complete the following short exercises to get a better sense of who you are. For examples and templates, see the *Finding Your Glasses Workbook* or go to the *Additional Resources* section of the website.

*Personal SWOT Analysis:*

In a personal SWOT Analysis you analyze your Strengths, Weaknesses, Opportunities, and Threats. Your Strengths and Weaknesses are internal (things that you can control) while Opportunities and Threats are external (things you cannot control).

*What Makes You Happy*

What are the things in your life that really enjoy? What are the things that put a smile on your face? Who are the people that you genuinely enjoy being around?

*Experiences that Shape You*

What are the major events that have shaped who you are? How have those events impacted you? Life is made up of an intricate mixing of experiences that have a great impact on who we are, but we still have the power to choose how we will allow it affect us long-term.

Understanding the real you and knowing your core values is a life long process. Before I married my wife, family was not one of my first look core values, but now it is number two in my life. Different events in your life may shape some of your core values and the understanding of the real you, so don't stop here. Continue on this journey for the rest of your life.

---

## ✔ ACTION ITEMS:

1. Send an email to your three closest friends or family members. Ask them to rate what they think your most important core values are. Compare the results to how you ranked your core values, and talk with them about the differences.

2. Do a short intro to who you are and answer the following questions (like an elevator pitch):
   a. Who am I really?
   b. Where do I add value?
   c. What excites me in life?
   d. What is my passion?

3. What are the top seven things that bring you the most enjoyment in life?

4. What are the top seven stressors in your life?

5. Don't forget to share with someone else in 24 hours what you have learned from this chapter.

# The "I" Exam

## CHAPTER THREE:
# A PREVIEW OF THE CLARIFYING CYCLE OF SUCCESS MODEL

*"Some people dream of success…while others wake up and work hard at it."*
— Unknown

---

## *" A Journey of Leadership "*

One day, I was feeling extremely depressed. I had just been through a very rough time in my life. I decided to read the book *Rich Dad, Poor Dad* by Robert Kiyosaki. While reading, I noticed a question that I never heard before. "What would I be willing to do for free?" I was willing enough to answer, so I wrote down my answers: leadership development, resume writing, and interview training. I had no idea that this would assist me in my own journey of finding my glasses.

After graduation I went to work for a major retailer. Throughout the interview process the manager mentioned how important leadership was to the company. This immediately resonated with me. I began working as a store manager, leading a team of 50 people. These were people of all ages, education backgrounds, and interests. It was a challenging but positive experience.

In order to be the best, I worked 60 to 80 hours a week to prove that I could turn the store around. Unfortunately, these long hours were beginning to affect my new marriage. After some conversations with my wife, I decided that this job was not the best for me.

The day after I quit this major retailer, I drove to Connecticut to attend a Golden Key Leadership Regional Training Conference. I was given the opportunity to lead a workshop that I developed called *Can You Manage to LEAD?* After the workshop students were gleefully standing in line waiting to talk with me. Many of them expressed that my leadership workshop was one of the best they ever attended. I received a lot of requests to present at other events.

There was one young lady that asked me a life-changing question. She asked, "Would you write your prices on the back of your business card?" Internally I wondered what she meant by prices. I had driven to the conference by myself. I stayed with my best friend in New York to decrease lodging expenses. Money was the furthest thing from my mind. I was leading this workshop because it was my passion. I let her know that I could work with her and her budget. Leaving that conference I realized that what I loved about leadership was speaking and training, and I realized that I was asking myself the wrong question. The question was not "Not what would I do for free?" Rather, the question was "What am I already doing for free?" I went to my best friend's house in New York and started my company that very same day.

I realized that if I was going to build a successful business, I needed to know the inner workings of how a training and development organization worked. I jumped at an opportunity to be a training coordinator for a financial investments firm in

Baltimore. I learned the how-to's of training and development during this experience. I continued to fill in areas where I could grow my passion by getting my MBA. My business continued to grow.

Now I am speaking at colleges, companies, and high schools about leadership and related topics. Although I am getting closer to what authentic success looks like for me, it will be a journey that I am consistently traveling. I am continually clarifying what my authentic career looks like. What about you? What does your journey look like? Are you getting closer to your authentic success?

## THE CLARIFYING CYCLE OF SUCCESS MODEL

It is time to not only dream, but to wake up and achieve those dreams! It is time to actually live a life that is both balanced (the way you define it) and enjoyable! I am not suggesting that everyone will get everything they ever wanted. I am also not saying that all you have to do is simply think about success and it will appear. What I am saying is that we can achieve more than we thought was ever possible. We can make a difference in the lives of more people than we ever thought, and we can actually achieve authentic success. Isn't your life worth it?

The *Clarifying Cycle of Success* model was birthed out of a desire to help others on their journey. It is a result of personal experiences and extensive research. I wanted to create a simple and practical process that would reveal what authentic success looks like and to help people actually achieve it. By following this model, you will be able to pursue your purpose, passions, and priorities. You will see that the model consists of the *6 Basic Lenses of Success*.

Even though the journey of authentic success is not an easy one, this model will help provide structure to a journey that is illusive to many. In Exhibit 3.1 you will see a brief description of the lenses that make up the model. Chapters 4 to 9 will go into more detail about the lenses and how to apply each lens within the cycle.

**Exhibit 3.1**

| The 6 Basic Lenses of Success: **R.E.T.I.N.A.** | | |
|---|---|---|
| Lens 1 | **R**eflective Thinking | Helps you to think through what you have been through, where you are now, and what you really want in life. This lens will allow you the time to |

| | | |
|---|---|---|
| | | press "pause" and really examine your life in order to move forward. |
| Lens 2 | **E**mpowering Vision | Helps you to see where you are going, and understand the importance of getting there. Without this lens you won't get a clear picture of where you would like to go in all areas of your life. |
| Lens 3 | **T**argeted Planning | Helps you to plot out the steps to achieving your empowering vision. While some believe in just winging it, this lens can help you save your time, resources, and frustration in order to get as close to your vision as possible. |
| Lens 4 | **I**nspiring ACTion | Helps you to do something with the targeted plans that you created. Without this step you will never get out of the vicious nightmare of should have's, could have's and would have's. |
| Lens 5 | **N**agging Persistence | Helps you to overcome the inevitable obstacles that occur while achieving authentic success. Without this lens you will give up too |

| | | |
|---|---|---|
| | | early on what you really want in life. |
| Lens 6 | **A**ppreciative Celebration | Helps you to appreciate the journey. There are many times when we do not achieve the intended vision, but this lens helps you to see what you have actually gained from the experience. Without this lens you might not see how far you have come, and who has helped you along the way. |

---

**REFLECTION EXERCISE 3.1**

How do you measure on the 6 Basic Lenses of Success? Please rate yourself (1 being the lowest and 5 being the highest) on how well these lenses are currently used in you life Write your number next to the lens.

Lens 1 – Reflective Thinking     _____    Ch. 4
Lens 2 – Empowering Vision     _____    Ch. 5
Lens 3 – Targeted Planning     _____    Ch. 6
Lens 4 – Inspiring ACTion     _____    Ch. 7
Lens 5 – Nagging Persistence     _____    Ch. 8
Lens 6 – Appreciative Celebration     _____    Ch. 9

---

## HOW TO USE THIS MODEL

The core value areas in our lives are usually very intertwined. Many areas impact other areas. For example, you might have more energy to use going back to school if you exercised and were healthier. While you may be tempted to work on everything at once, I would caution you against doing that as you can become overwhelmed. You may also be tempted to work on only one area, and I would caution you against as well. Focusing on only one area may cause detriment in other areas without careful consideration. I encourage you to focus on three areas at a time. Most of the time, people focus on the first look areas first. The reason I chose three areas is that people can usually focus on three areas without getting overwhelmed.

Please note that while you may be focused on these areas in your life, it does not mean that you can neglect the other areas of your life. For example, even though Exercise is in my Third Look core value category, I am still working toward becoming more fit. I coach my clients to improve all aspects of their lives, but trying to improve everything at once can be challenging, and if not accomplished, disheartening. Start off with a manageable process. I believe in the saying, "Rome was not built in a day." Neither is authentic success!

Even though you will focus on only three areas, there may be one of greater importance than the others, like your primary core value. When I really began the process of finding my glasses, much of it centered on the core value of faith. As a Christian, I wanted to make sure that I was clear on what I believed and what impact that would have on the other areas of my life. Other people have focused on their individual faiths, family, career, health, or any of the other areas. Either way, you will see great progress in your life. The great thing is that when you start improving in one area, it usually impacts other areas of your life.

After you get to the *Inspiring ACTion* lens of each of the three areas, then you should bring your Second Look core values into focus. Doing this will help you to gain momentum in your life.

Once you are moving in a positive direction, you will notice that it will be easier to focus on other areas in your life.

You can also start wherever you are in the process. One of the individuals I was working with had already gone through reflection and empowering vision without even talking to me. If you realize that you have already completed one of the lenses, just start where you feel is right. Whatever you do, please make sure that you have done a thorough job on *Reflective Thinking*. The *Relfective Thinking* lens is about what you really want based on your core values, so give that stage the appropriate amount of time and effort.

The *Clarifying Cycle of Success Model* is continuous and really never ends. I will continue to clarify what authentic success looks like for me as I continue to grow, experience new things, and see what happens in the other core value areas of my life. This may be affected by my wife and having several children, a close friend going through a very traumatic time in his life, or something else. The important thing is to keep going through the model. You will see the more you go through the model the more natural it will become. In the following chapters you will receive information to help you through this process.

I want to remind you that you can do this. Sometimes the hardest thing to do is start. Once you get started it becomes easier and easier! If you have gotten this far, I know you are committed and can continue revealing and achieving. Know that the race is not given to whoever is the fastest, but it is given to those that endure to the very end. I believe that you can endure to the very end!

---

## ✓ ACTION ITEMS:

---

1. Decide what three core value areas you will focus on. Usually the First Look core values are used here. Share this with a close family member or friend.
2. As you go through the model, pick one core value that you will focus on, as it can help you in your learning process.
3. Write down which areas of the *Clarifying Cycle of Success Model* that you usually do, and the areas that you rarely do. Then write down why you feel that is the case.
4. Don't forget to share with someone else in 24 hours what you have learned from this chapter.

A Preview of the Clarifying Cycle of Success Model

# CHAPTER FOUR:
## LENS 1 – REFLECTIVE THINKING:
## WHO/WHAT HAVE I BEEN

*"By three methods we may learn wisdom. First, by reflection, which is the noblest; second, by imitation which is the easiest; and third by experience, which is the bitterest"* – Confucius

---

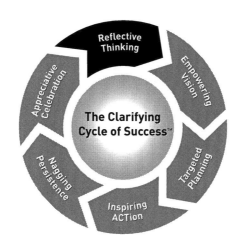

*" Overweight and on a Ranch"*

### Sophia Franklin

Being at The Biggest Loser Ranch challenged Sophia to reflect on her life and how she had gained so much weight. This was a life changing moment for her, and this was an exciting change for the better.

> When my brother passed away it really hurt. He was a huge part of my life and his death changed a lot for me. I tried to immerse myself in everything else to keep busy, but underneath it all was a deep hurt that led to much of my weight gain. I knew I had to deal with this. I had to face my life and determine what I wanted it to look like. Some of the biggest challenges for me have been self-sabotage and doubt, but as I look forward I am willing to go against the norm to be genuinely happy.

Sophia's time of reflection was an extraordinary opportunity, but even then she could have chosen to not confront the issues keeping her from authentic success. Through her process she has come to a greater sense of peace and has shifted to her authentic self. We should follow Sophia's actions and take time to confront our true selves.

## WHY REFLECTIVE THINKING

When was the last time you sat down and did absolutely nothing? Dr. Brownstein, a former professor of mine, encouraged me to do this. I also encourage you to do the same. Take 60 seconds to do absolutely nothing. Try not to think about anything. It may take some time to get used to, but it is worth it. It is a very serene experience. We have been conditioned to always do something. It can feel really good to do nothing! I believe you can do absolutely nothing and actually love it!

*Webster's Dictionary* defines reflection:

1. A thought, idea, or opinion formed or a remark made as a result of meditation.
2. Consideration of some subject matter, idea, or purpose.

Reflective Thinking is the first lens in the *Clarifying Cycle of Success Model*. It is the ability to analyze one's life in such away to produce a clearer understanding of one's past. Reflective Thinking allows you ponder how things have been going in your life. With this lens it is imperative that you are honest with yourself. Without honesty you will not be able to effectively move forward.

## REFLECTION EXERCISE 4.1

How often do you reflect on your life? What are some ways that you reflect in your everyday life? What are some reasons that you have not reflected as much as you would like?

_____

_____

_____

_____

_____

_____

_____

_____

_____

_____

_____

Reflective Thinking is especially important in today's fast-paced society. With so many things to do we can get sucked into always being busy. We lose the ability to simply "be." What I mean by simply "being" is to press pause in order to understand ourselves and understand how things have affected us.

I believe there are many different reasons that people do not think reflectively their lives. Some want to, but never create the time or the space in order to do it. Some have never learned how to think reflectively and therefore never do it. Some do not because they are concerned with what they will find. In the *Road Less Traveled*, M. Scott Peck shares how examining the world outside of us is never as painful as examining the world within. He also shares that people stay away from genuine self-examination for fear of what they will find, or unleashing what they already know.

There are two different types of Reflective Thinking: Informal and Formal. Informal Reflective Thinking is when you happen to have an unplanned thought about how things are going in your life. Formal Reflective Thinking involves having a scheduled time to think about your life or a specific area in your life. I try my best to schedule a time for reflective thinking each quarter to make sure I am moving in the right direction.

There are several benefits to Reflective Thinking. One benefit is that it helps you to learn from your mistakes. If you are like me, you have committed the same errors over and over and over again. I have had relationships that ended in the same result simply because I never changed.

Another benefit to Reflective Thinking is that it gives you great ideas. In times of Reflective Thinking I usually think about solutions to problems that I had not considered before.

A third benefit is that it helps you to help others. When you realize that what you are experiencing can help others, you start to think about ways to include others. For example, one of my goals is to run a marathon. Initially it was going to only be my friend Gerrod and me. Then I realized that I should extend the opportunity to other people. Why not involve other people and raise money for a great cause? Now we have a team of 5 people with a goal to raise $5,000 to give people access to clean water through the organization *charity: water*.

Benefit 4 is that it makes you happier. When you think about how much you have progressed in an area in your life, it can have a positive mental impact. You realize the momentum that is building in your life.

Finally, a fifth benefit is that it helps to give you the right perspective. I remember going to Africa for the first time to visit my family (my dad is from Ghana). I remember taking a shower in the village where he grew up, and I had to heat up the water and put it in a bucket. It made me realize how much I took running water for granted! That experience changed my perspective. When I engaged in Reflective Thinking I walked away with a new mantra in life – *There are people who would love to have my bad days!* Because we live life on fast-forward, we can miss out on the little things that make a big difference.

---

## REFLECTION EXERCISE 4.2

Which of the benefits listed above is the top reason you would like spend time in Reflective Thinking?

| | | |
|---|---|---|
| Benefit 1 | Helps you learn from your mistakes. | _____ |
| Benefit 2 | It gives you great ideas. | _____ |
| Benefit 3 | It helps you to help others. | _____ |
| Benefit 4 | It makes you happier. | _____ |
| Benefit 5 | It gives you the right perspective. | _____ |

---

## SELF-AWARENESS

 *Tim Kassouf: A DUI in life.*

Tim looked in his rear view mirror. He dreaded what he saw. It was the blinding light of a police car. He was being pulled over and he had a pretty good idea why. Tim was charged with DUI (Driving Under the Influence).

> That event caused me to do some serious reflection. I realized that I was 50 lbs heavier then I used to be, I was in major credit card debt, and I had not been to church in 2 years. I was not living up to the most important values of my faith, and I knew it. From that moment I was determined to change!

Tim did change. He is now fit, doing well financially, and he leads a youth group at his church. It is unfortunate that it took the DUI to wake him up to change, but sometimes that is what it takes. Let this moment be your DUI. Challenge yourself to look into the mirror and to see the great importance of Reflective Thinking.

Being self-aware is essential to Reflective Thinking. When we are not self-aware we do not see what everyone else sees about us. Have you ever encountered a person at work or school who had a problem, and everyone around him or her knew they had a problem, but for some reason she or he had no idea he or she had a problem? We develop self-awareness through times of Reflective Thinking.

When you are self-aware you realize certain mindsets that you have, such as the "one-more-thing" mentality. In *Your Authentic Self*, Ric Giardina discusses this mentality. It occurs when people says, "Let me get this one last thing completed, and then I'll slow down and take a break." Sometimes people are doing "one more thing" for hours more with no intention of stopping. Some of the negative effects of the one-more-thing mentality are:

1. We stop taking care of ourselves, which is bad for the body, spirit, and emotions.
2. We continually break our word.
3. If we do not complete one more thing consistently we do not feel like we have done enough.

If we are not self-aware we may be living by the one-more-thing mentality and minimizing our times of Reflective Thinking. Self-awareness can lead to an increase in self-knowledge. Without self-knowledge there can be no authentic success, no authentic happiness, and no authentic living. If we do not know who we are then how can we really know what success is? This is one of the main reasons we copy others, because we do not take the time out to figure out whom we are. Without understanding who we are as individuals, we conform to the identity of others. We then measure our success to the person or ideology we have copied.

---

### REFLECTION EXERCISE 4.3

On a scale from 1 to 5 (with 1 being the lowest and 5 being the highest) how well do you know yourself? Why have you rated yourself this way?

---

## USING REFLECTIVE THINKING

There are many ways to think reflectively. One great way to is to journal. For a large portion of my life I journaled every day. My journal was the one place that I could be totally honest about my feelings. It is a good thing to be able to unload on a piece of paper.

Sometimes I read over my old journal and it amazes me how much I have progressed. You can write in an online journal such as www.penzu.com. You can write in a journal book daily or at any specified interval you decide. You can also record a voice journal where you say your thoughts and feelings into a recording device.

Taking time out every day to think reflectively is also very beneficial. Consciously decide that before you go to bed you will spend a few minutes looking over your day and how it could have been improved. Thinking about your day can help you get all of those thoughts out so that you can focus on actually going to sleep.

Exercising is also a great way to think reflectively. I recently spoke at a conference, before I was scheduled to speak I worked out in the hotel recreation room. I was running on the treadmill as fast as my little legs could take me, but one thing I noticed was that I thought about a lot that was going on in my life. I made a very important decision on what I would do to improve my faith walk. It was a refreshing moment.

Reflective Thinking can also be beneficial when you share it with those you trust. This person can be a spouse, a best friend, or an accountability partner. It is always good to have someone else that you can be transparent with and bounce what you are really saying and feeling off of.

I believe it is helpful to have tools to use during times of Formal Reflective Thinking. The *Plus/Delta* is a very simple tool. If you ever want to do this on your own, all you have to do is draw a line down the middle of a piece of paper. On the left side write "Plus" and on the right side write "Delta." The "Plus" side asks the question, "What am I doing well?" The "Delta" side asks, "What do I need to change?"

## REFLECTION EXERCISE 4.4

Think reflectively about your life last week. What did you do well and what could you improve?

| Plus (+) | Delta (Δ) |
| --- | --- |
| | |

The Four Stage Analysis Model is another simple tool to use, which I learned from Martin Kormanik. It asks four simple questions:

1. Where am I now?
2. Where do I want to be?
3. What are the barriers preventing me from getting there?
4. How do I remove those barriers?

This tool can be used for both your overall life and specific areas within your life.

---

### REFLECTION EXERCISE 4.5

Please answer the following four questions for a specific area in your life. What is that area? _____

1. Where am I now?


2. Where do I want to be?


3. What are the barriers preventing me from getting there?


4. How do I remove those barriers?

---

I encourage you to implement this first lens and take time to think reflectively. It can help you learn from your mistakes, process the events your life, and ultimately move forward. You are very fortunate, because if you are reading this right now you have the opportunity to improve your life. You do not have to repeat the same mistakes. This is your moment to make a decision to move forward through Reflective Thinking.

## ✔ ACTION ITEMS:

1. Set your Formal Reflective Thinking schedule (monthly, quarterly, annually) and put it on your calendar.
2. Decide how you want to capture your daily progress (journaling, Plus/Delta, or another method).
3. Write down a time when you have used Reflective Thinking. How did it benefit you?
4. Don't forget to share with someone else in 24 hours what you have learned from this chapter.

# Lens 1 – Refletive Thinking

# CHAPTER FIVE:
# LENS 2 – EMPOWERING VISION:
# WHERE AM I GOING?

*"Where there is no vision, the people perish"* – Proverbs 29:18a

---

*" Eradicating Sex-trafficking by Making Noise"*

### Okey and Leslie Nwoke

While sitting in Okey and Leslie Nwoke's apartment in Washington, DC, I could tell that this would be a special interview. Okey and Leslie have a unique passion. "We help make noise about the social injustices occurring in the world, especially human trafficking," they said. Leslie saw the beginnings of this vision at an early age.

> I received the calling to make a major difference in this area when I was 13. I realized this even more on a trip to Honduras during my junior year of college. I didn't see it all, but I knew that I had to do something. I couldn't wait until it all came together perfectly.

Together, the couple began Making Noise Incorporated, a non-profit organization that aims to use the arts, media, drama, and blogs to raise awareness of social injustice issues in the continent of Africa. They had a vision for change, and put action to their vision. The Nwokes started showing a documentary they created after a trip to Uganda, and the rest is history.

They believe in their vision, and it is so empowering that others have partnered with them to change the world. The Nwokes recalled a quote they heard over the years: "Those people who are crazy enough to believe they can change the world are the ones who end up doing it."

## EMPOWERING VISION DEFINED

After you have determined where you have been, it is important to state where you are going. I have seen too many people wander around trying to find their way through life only wake up wondering where they are. Don't waste another minute wondering.

Have you ever really wanted something? Think back to when you were a kid. Was there one piece of candy that you always wanted? I always wanted a Butterfinger. Now fast-forward to today. There are things that I want in life and I can see myself accomplishing them. There are things that you can accomplish if you try. There are people's lives you can change if you put in the effort. Just like that piece of candy that you always wanted as a child - at some point you finally ate it. You may still eat it today, but you achieved that vision. Are you willing to achieve one that is much bigger now?

*Webster's Dictionary* defines vision:
1. A thought, concept, or object formed by the imagination.
2. Mode of seeing or conceiving.

What is your imagination seeing based on your core values? Does it empower you? An empowering vision is something that not only excites you, but it also excites other people. However, the most important part of this equation is you. You need to be excited and encouraged to actually achieve what is formed by your imagination.

Having a vision is very important as it denotes the direction in which you are headed and the destination you intend to reach. Imagine that you are driving to a new city. You know that it is south of where you currently are, but that is all you know in terms of directions. If you don't know exactly where you are going, how will you ever know if you were successful in getting there? It may be wise to ask for help, but even then the directions that people give won't help you arrive at your destination. What if you had your destination already programmed into the GPS? This keen sense of direction is why having a vision is so important.

---

**🎯 REFLECTION EXERCISE 5.1**
What is the importance of having a vision to you?
Write down your answers.

_____

_____

_____

_____

_____

_____

---

## CREATING A VISION STATEMENT

Do you have a vision statement? When I first heard about writing a vision statement, I thought it was a bunch of motivational nonsense. After continuing to hear about it from reputable sources, I decided to give it a try. As a result of writing a vision statement, I am moving faster toward the direction of my written vision. I feel like I have been able to achieve more of it than before.

Your vision is important in identifying where you are going. It is like your personal GPS. It can serve as a guiding light in a dark world that can be a hindrance to positive growth and ultimate achievement. Without a vision, the life you were supposed to live may perish!

These are some helpful tips in creating a vision statement:

- You can have one main vision statement or several for the different areas of your life.

- This is not a step-by-step plan, but a description of what your future success will look like.
- Write the vision statement in first person, as if you are already doing it. For example, "I am an international speaker inspiring millions on how to apply ACTion to their everyday lives."
- Your vision statement should include your First Look Core Values at a minimum.

Answer the following questions to help establish your vision:

1. What would you do for free for the rest of your life?

2. What would you try to accomplish if you were guaranteed that you would not fail?

3. What are the five top things that you enjoy doing the most?

4. What are your strengths?

5. What are the most important areas in your life (i.e. physical, spiritual, work or career, family, social relationships, financial security, mental improvement and attention, education, or fun)?

Here is a sample of my vision statement: "*I am inspiring a new generation of global leaders to 'THINK. BELIEVE. ACT!' I am doing this by being a loving husband and father, a down-to-earth college professor, author, international speaker, media personality, an out the box pastor at a multicultural ministry. I am keeping my energy up to do all this by eating healthy, exercising regularly, and reading often.*

**REFLECTION EXERCISE 5.2**

What should be the key elements (core values, things to accomplish, people to include) of your vision statement? Are these key elements exciting to you?

_____

_____

_____

_____

_____

_____

_____

_____

### Myrtis Bedolla: Sight for Good Eyes

Myrtis, the owner of Galerie Myrtis, was a part of a marketing campaign for the American Physical Therapy Association. She was driving 45 minutes to and from work. When one of her sons was injured, she knew something had to change. She desired to be closer to her children in their time of need. It was this great attitude that helped her start her business.

The effect of one's attitude is paramount. What we say to ourselves is what we manifest. It is what we become. So in essence it pushes out our vision. Overall, I desire family over great wealth and I seek to have a life enriched by a great family and travel. My vision will always reflect that.

Myrtis is making an impact in the world of contemporary fine arts. It all started with a simple vision to do what she was passionate about doing, and to be closer to her family. She acknowledges the great importance that vision had and continues to have on her life.

---

### ● REFLECTION EXERCISE 5.3

Has your life been guided by a clear vision of where you are going? Why or why not?

_____

_____

_____

_____

_____

_____

_____

---

You must understand the reason that you have a vision. I have seen countless people create vision statements that sound great, but they cannot fully articulate the why. Understanding the why starts with knowledge of your core values. In my vision statement all of my First Look Core Values are included (Faith, Family, and Career).

I would like to accomplish my vision because I want to make a positive difference in this world. I want to first start with my family and then others that I am afforded the opportunity to inspire. What is your why? Why do you want to accomplish your vision? What does it really mean to you?

Another piece that sometimes is forgotten in establishing a vision is the feeling. Understanding how you would feel if you accomplished your vision is a giant part of the momentum necessary to keep you moving forward. Even if you do not have a clearly written vision statement yet, is there something on your heart to accomplish? Take a moment and just think how it would feel if you were to accomplish that! Seriously, *stop reading for a moment and just spend 60 seconds to visualize yourself achieving it.*

How did you feel? You probably have a smile on your face right now. There is something about seeing and experiencing the feelings of achieving our vision that brings forth smiles. Sometimes I visualize my wife and myself getting out of debt. I picture our sending in the last check to Sallie Mae for our student loans and I get excited. I also think of sending that last check to the mortgage company for our house and just rolling around in the grass with joy. This helps me stay motivated along the journey to keep moving forward with intense efforts. Another way to stay motivated is to keep your vision in front of you. Put it on your smartphone screen saver or put it on a note card. Make a conscious effort to read it often.

Keep in mind that your vision is subject to change as you continue to go through life. Events or people may affect your vision, causing you to adjust it. As I continue to clarify what authentic success looks like for me it causes me to update my vision. Do not feel locked in to what you originally create as your vision statement. On the other hand, do not let obstacles steer you off the path of achieving your vision. You will learn more about overcoming obstacles in Chapter 8.

### *Samuel Smith: A Passion for the Future.*

I met Samuel at the University of Pittsburgh while speaking at a conference. Samuel is a person that I will never forget. After the presentation he asked questions that let me know that he was really paying attention. He actually followed up with me after the conference. What I could tell about Samuel was that he was very intentional in what he was doing. He cared enough about his vision for the future to ask questions and sought advice on how to bring it to pass.

Samuel let me know that eventually he wanted to own his own business. He received an amazing internship that summer that gave him the desire to be an entrepreneur. This experience fueled his drive to do well. "I try not to waste time on trivial things," Samuel said. "I still have a lot of fun, but I make sure that I complete my assignments and the things I have set out to do with excellence." Samuel is on his way to a future filled with authentic success. He has a clear vision of where he wants to go, why he wants to go there, and what it will feel like when he gets there. What about you?

## FOCUSED VISION

Having focus with vision is essential to staying on track. We need the kind of focus that a horse has right before a race. Many times you will see the horses with blinders on to keep them focused on the track ahead instead the horses next to them. We need to be careful not to compare ourselves to others around us.

Focus is also needed regarding our core values. We have to remember what is important to us and what really matters in life. A close friend's wife died recently. I could have said to him, "I am sorry, but I am focused on writing my book right now." I stayed with him for a week and did not resume writing until I arrived back home. Spending time with him was more important to me than finishing my book, even though I had looming deadlines.

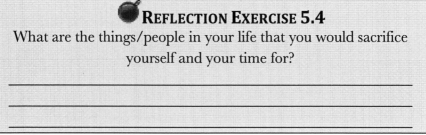

**REFLECTION EXERCISE 5.4**

What are the things/people in your life that you would sacrifice yourself and your time for?

_____

_____

_____

If you have a vision with your core values as a filter then you are on the right track toward authentic success. I believe that as you set the vision for your life or even specific areas in your life that you will achieve more of what you are looking for in life. I encourage you to write down your vision, because when you write it out it becomes etched in your brain even more. Isn't your life important enough to focus on creating a direction for your life? You don't have to wander around aimlessly.

In the next chapter you will learn how to create a plan on how to actualize your vision. Ready, Aim, and Fire!

## ACTION ITEMS:

1. Write out the vision statement for your life (for more information on creating a vision statement see the _Additional Resources_ section of the website).
2. Share your vision statement with a close family member or friend. Share why you want to accomplish it and the feelings that you would have if you did.
3. Help other people that you know write a vision statement. Spend some time walking them through how to create one.
4. Don't forget to share with someone else in 24 hours what you have learned from this chapter.

# CHAPTER SIX:
## LENS 3 – TARGETED PLANNING:
## HOW WILL I GET THERE?

*"By failing to prepare, you are preparing to fail."* – Benjamin Franklin

*" Silicon Valley is Not Good Enough"*

## *Larry Fiorino:*

L arry was very successful. He was working for a billion-dollar company as the National Vice President of Technology. The company was doing so well that it moved to Silicon Valley in California, and they wanted Larry to move with them. He decided that he did not want to uproot his family, so he started his own company with a laptop and a cell phone.

> My wife was the first investor in the company. Her commitment, a growing family, and the utilization of technology all were a part of the planning process for G.1440. All of this pushed me to action.

There were people who said that he could not have his own company and that he would fail. The odds were against him. However, he made a conscious decision to ignore it all. During our interview Larry said something that stood out. He said, "You have to know what is important to you and follow that. Success will come." Larry saw the benefits of moving to California with the company, but the cost for his family was too high. This was not the plan he would choose.  He stayed in Maryland and has both a successful family and profitable business.

## TARGETED PLANNING DEFINED

Have you ever done something important without a plan? If you are like me then it didn't work out as well as it could have. Early on in my speaking career I went to speak at a college. I had a vision for what I wanted to talk about. Unfortunately, I didn't have a plan about how I would structure my speech. It was a disaster. I fumbled over words and I'm fortunate that I managed to get through it. I didn't get positive feedback, but I vowed that that experience would be my first and last.

Targeted Planning is the third lens in the *Clarifying Cycle of Success Model*. This lens will help you map out how you will get to your destination. In the last chapter we talked about the empowering vision as the destination. Targeted Planning provides the actual directions to reach the destination. It is planning with a specific target in mind.

Targeted Planning is very important to authentic success. Many people have great visions, but act upon them with no real plan to get there. They end up spending much of their time trying to figure out what went wrong, versus inputting minor course corrections along their journey. In 1956, Earl Nightingale wrote, "The strangest secret is that we become what we think about most of the time." This is true as it relates to planning, because what we plan is usually what we see.

### Brenda Young: Planning for Success

Brenda Young is a fifty-eight year old mother of four adult sons. Thirty years ago she became a single parent and entered the world of work, but soon discovered she couldn't give her children the lifestyle she felt they deserved. She didn't have a college education. An opportunity for change presented itself through a state-funded training program in technology. This launched her career in technology training and education, which continued over the next twenty years. Brenda has worked with three different companies and various senior level management positions.

As her children grew into adulthood, she sustained long working hours, presenting ideas to CEOs and presidents of companies. She assessed training and project management needs of international organizations and built training programs to meet those needs. Moreover, they were willing to pay substantially for these solutions. This gave her children the lifestyle she wanted for them.

However, Brenda doubted her credibility. After all, she did not have the credentials to justify this life. Her contributions seemed superficial. The financial rewards didn't equate to *authentic success*.

Ten years ago, she stepped down from this twenty-year career to assess herself. After six months and much consideration, she accepted a teaching position at a residential training facility for high-risk youth where she could use her needs assessment skills to guide students through major life changes. Here she could add value to human lives, and it proved to be rewarding. Over time, the doubt of her credibility crept back into her life. She was asking of her students what she had not yet done for herself, to get a college education.

In March 2008, Brenda enrolled in college and, in May 2010, completed her Associates degree. She will complete her Bachelor's degree in Communications in 2012. Throughout this time, she continues to work with at-risk young adult students helping them realize their potential. After many years, she likens herself to the main character of one of her favorite children's books *The Velveteen Rabbit*. The Velveteen Rabbit says, "My fur is mostly worn off and my joints are getting old, but that is what makes me real." Adding value to human lives is truly *authentic success*.

It is evident that Brenda aligned her planning with her vision, and was willing to do what was necessary to get there, while being conscious of her core values along the way. Brenda inspired me as she discussed her planning and actions to get to her current level of happiness.

**REFLECTION EXERCISE 6.1**

Relfect on the past year of your life. How often did you achieve your goals?

_____

_____

# R.E.A.L. GOALS ™

It is generally accepted that goal setting is very useful to accomplishing your vision. In _48 Days To the Work You Love_, Dan Miller shares that only 8% of the population identifies with writing clear goals. There have been different methods to create goals. Locke's Goal Setting Theory uses the S.M.A.R.T. Method (Specific, Measurable, Attainable, Realistic, and Timely). The major difference between R.E.A.L. Goals ™ and S.M.A.R.T. goals is addressing the question of why and establishing the emotional connection with the goal. That is accomplished through R.E.A.L. Goals. I ventured to create something that was pertinent to this specific project, but still captured the most important elements of the different bodies of work on goal setting.

R.E.A.L. Goals ™ stand for goals that are Reachable, Explicit, Attractive, and Length-conscious.

**Exhibit 6.1**

| R.E.A.L. Goals ™ | |
|---|---|
| **R**eachable | Achievable (both willing and able) yet stretch goals. Not too many at once. |
| **E**xplicit | Clear, specific, and measurable |
| **A**ttractive | The why of the goal, the emotional connection, and the reward |
| **L**ength-Conscious | Has a specified end date/time |

Reachable goals are goals that a person can reasonably accomplish. When people set goals that are not reachable they usually end up with increased frustration and a loss of motivation. However, the goals should not be so easy that it does not take hard work to achieve them. Even though the goals are reachable, they should also be challenging.

Explicit goals are clear, specific, and measurable. The more specific a goal is the less likely ambiguity will erode the chances of completing it. For example, instead of saying "I will run twice a week", say you will run on Tuesdays and Thursdays of each week. When your goals are explicit it is much easier to be held accountable and to determine if you have actually accomplished your goals or not.

Attractive goals answer two main questions: Why is this goal important for you to achieve? How would you feel if you accomplished this goal? It is important to establish why a goal is important to achieve because it increases the likelihood of you achieving it. The same thing is accomplished when an emotional connection is established between you and the goal that you set. You should also plan a reward for yourself for achieving that goal. Be careful that the reward does not detract from your intended goal. If you are trying to lose weight, don't eat a whole chocolate cake as a reward, perhaps just a small slice instead.

Length-conscious goals have a specified end date/time. Not allowing the goal to go on forever can help to achieve the goal. Without being conscious about the deadline there may not be a sense of urgency to complete the goal.

An example of a R.E.A.L. Goal™ would be this: "I will start my own business developing websites within six months in order to do what I'm passionate about and to get out of debt. I will feel both excited and relieved to start my new company. This is much more precise than stating, "I want to make more money."

Setting goals is not a one-time event. It is an ongoing process of rewiring the brain. It is generally accepted that it takes 21-30 days to form a habit, and this has been proven to be fairly accurate on a neurological basis as new neural patterns are formed after something is repeated enough times.

You can use R.E.A.L. Goals™ every day. You can either end your day with creating new goals for the next day or you can create new goals in the morning. These are considered short-term goals. Long-term goals have more long-range approach and may take you a year or more to accomplish.

About three years ago I sat down and created three R.E.A.L. Goals™. My three goals were to write my first book within a year, to have my own radio show in three years, and be in business for myself in three years. I accomplished writing the book within a year, I had my own radio show after only eight months and three years later I'm now in business for myself full-time.

---

### REFLECTION EXERCISE 6.2

Which of the four areas of R.E.A.L. (Reachable, Explicit, Attractive, and Length-conscious) is the most relevant to you? How would setting R.E.A.L. Goals™ change the way you currently approach goal setting?

_____

_____

_____

_____

_____

_____

Objectives are the specifics of how you will achieve the R.E.A.L. Goals™ you are setting. For example, let's say that someone wants to spend more time with his or her family. They decide to create the goal of having a monthly family weekend every first weekend of the month. An objective would be to plan out each weekend the week after the last family weekend. Another objective would be to create a family calendar so that the family can see what they will be doing for the upcoming family weekend. The objectives help to accomplish the R.E.A.L. Goals™.

## PROFESSIONAL ACCOUNTABILITY PARTNERS (PRAP™)

"Whoever isolates himself seeks his own desire; he breaks out against all sound judgment." – Ancient Hebrew Proverb

Accountability can positively impact your chances of achieving your goals and ultimately your authentic success. People tend to do better when they go to the gym with a partner; there is a continuing trend for people to progress more in their faith with a spiritual accountability partner. Surprisingly, goal achievement is relatively low. This can be seen by several studies on New Year's Resolutions. Research from the Opinion Corporation of Princeton, NJ, found that only 8% of people who set New Year's Resolutions are always successful at achieving them; 49% of people have infrequent success and 24% of people never succeed. A different study by proactivechange.com showed how resolutions are maintained over time. 75% of people maintain their resolutions past the first week, 71% past the 2nd week, 64% past one month, and only 46% past six months. With the low achievement, it is clear that greater levels of accountability are needed.

The term PrAP™ (Professional Accountability Partners) was created after I collaborated with my friend, Bismarck McCauley.

We wondered if the same principle that is attached to people who have spiritual accountability partners would work in our professional lives. We discussed the need for accountability regarding our vision and goals.

During the same time I found a study conducted by the American Society of Training in Development in 1998 on goal achievement, which led to PrAP™. The study focused on goal achievement. According to the research, if a person made a conscious decision to achieve a goal, 25% of people achieved it. If they said when the goal would be achieved, 40% achieved it. If they said how the goal would be achieved, 50% of achieved it. If they told someone else 65%, achieved it (see Exhibit 6.2)

**Exhibit 6.2**

Study on Goal Achievement

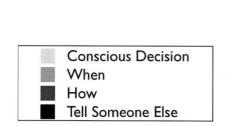

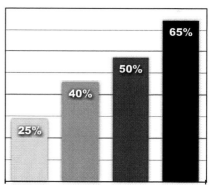

In order to set-up a successful PrAP™ system please heed the following steps:

**Step 1:** Seek out someone who you feel desires to grow professionally as much as you do. This person doesn't have to be in the same field or work for the same company. This person should be someone you aren't working with on a daily basis. Once you gain an initial agreement, proceed to the Expectation Meeting.

ACTion: Prepare expectations for expectation meeting. How often you will meet? Where you will meet? How long will your meetings be? Be detailed.

**Step 2:** Conduct an Expectation Meeting to determine if you will move forward with the person whom you have chosen as a potential PrAP.
ACTion: Prepare items for a Foundation meeting (Personal SWOT Analysis, 4 Stage Analysis Model, Vision Statement, R.E.A.L. Goals for 1, 3, and 10 years).

**Step 3:** Conduct a Foundation Meeting (1st official meeting as PrAP's).

ACTion: Complete the ACTion items that were determined during the Foundation Meeting.

**Step 4:** Conduct Regular PrAP Meetings.

ACTion: Complete the ACTion items and challenge your PrAP.

**Step 5**: Conduct Evaluation Meeting to measure your goal achievement efforts and to help increase effectiveness with your PrAP. This will assist you in deciding if this specific partnership should continue or if you should seek a different PrAP. This is usually conducted every six months or annually.

ACTion: Work on areas of improvement and complete the ACTion items set in a meeting.

**Step 6:** Continue Maximizing Your Effectiveness.

ACTion: Share the benefits of having a PrAP with someone else to help him or her maximize their effectiveness!

Here are some tips for your PrAP meetings:

1. Start each meeting with an update on progress of goals.
2. Take turns sharing updates and offer advice to the other person on some goals they can pursue.

3. Leave each meeting with no more than 3 ACTion items. Be sure to note what core values and goals the ACTion items connect to.

4. Work hard, but HAVE FUN!

## MENTORS, TIMELINES, AND MILESTONES

Not only are Professional Accountability Partners excellent in helping you achieve your vision, but mentors are also a great resource. Mentors can help avoid potential pitfalls, especially if they have achieved or are close to achieving the vision that you have set for yourself. Mentors that can share their mistakes with me and are willing to help me avoid them.

Mentors are also essential for dealing with "Lens 5 - Nagging Persistence," because they can help you understand the cycle of what you are achieving. For instance, a person decides that part of authentic success involves selling real estate. He or she starts in the fall and have very few clients by December. He or she may want to give up, but a mentor will share that it in that field it may take at least two years to be able to start making money.

One of my mentors helps me set realistic timelines for what I want to accomplish with my consulting/speaking career. Without his guidance, it would be rather challenging setting realistic timelines.

---

### REFLECTION EXERCISE 6.3

How has a mentor (formal or informal) helped you in the past?
How would having a consistent mentor help you now?

_____

_____

_____

_____

_____

_____

---

In this planning lens it is also valuable to create milestones. Milestones are steps in your progress that you have achieved and display your forward momentum. When I decided I would work full time for myself, this was a milestone that I set and achieved. Milestones can be as small as getting my first client to as big as making a certain dollar amount in the pursuit of accomplishing a goal. We will talk more about the achievement of milestones in Chapter 9.

## THE FRAME OF SACRIFICE AND THE COST/BENEFIT ANALYSIS

One thing that frustrated me for so many years was failure in achieving even the simplest goals in my life. I would set a vision, attach goals, and still never accomplish them. Have there been times in your life where it appeared that even the simplest of visions or goals continued to elude you? I have seen a constant trend in the people I have coached. That one thing can be seen through The Frame of Sacrifice.

For some reason, we think that we can just say we want to do something and it will happen. The Sacrifice Lens states that whenever we want something new to come into our lives, something old must come out. If you want to spend more time with your family that time has to come from somewhere. If you want to start your own business, that time and effort has to come from somewhere. For years I thought I could just think it and it would happen, but rarely did it ever happen. In the Frame of Sacrifice you write down, in the Targeted Planning, what you are willing to sacrifice (what goes out) in order to achieve your vision or R.E.A.L. Goals. What you sacrifice shouldn't conflict with your core values. If family is above career to you in core values, then family should not always be sacrificed for career. Rather career should be sacrificed more often for family.

### Justin and Stephanie Jones-Fosu: Debt and an Argument

In December of 2008, my wife and I had an argument. Because of the great debt we were in (over $125,000) not including the house, we decided to not get each other Christmas presents. I was the main person handling the finances at that time. One night Stephanie came home and stated that she would need money as she would be participating in Secret Santa at work. The cost would be up to $30. This perplexed me, as I wondered why we would get someone else a present when we were not getting presents for each other. This led to an argument because I wanted for us to stick to our agreement. She did not do secret santa (yeah!!!!).

I felt horrible after the argument, because I felt like a failure. At the time we were making roughly $75,000.00 but we were still living paycheck to paycheck. I felt I had two options. I could cry and mope, or I could get up and do something about it. Well, after I cried for a few moments I got up and did something about it. I went downstairs and looked at a book that I had in my library for several years, but never read. The book was called *The Total Money Makeover* by financial expert Dave Ramsey.

I was inspired to see where our money was going, and major light bulbs came on. Like most Americans, we were living beyond our means in credit card debt, hospital bills, and car payments. I scrutinized our bank statements and saw that we spent over $800.00 in non-grocery related food items. That consisted of me eating both breakfast and lunch almost every day at work, us eating out with friends regularly, and having little snacks here and there. Let me repeat, this had nothing to do with what we were spending for groceries. It was little things like this that brought the Sacrifice Lens into full perspective.

My wife read the book next and decided that we would need to sacrifice in order to reach our vision of not living paycheck to paycheck and eventually being debt free. We started making our lunches, stopped eating out as much with our friends, cut off our cable (we considered this a luxury when we added it up for the entire year), started living life on zero-based budget (where we figured out where all of our money would go before we spent any of it), sold one of our cars, and used all of our tax refund to pay debt.

Many people thought we were crazy, but they were also the ones who appeared to be comfortable being in debt. That year we eliminated $21,500.00 worth of debt from our lives; at this moment we only have student loans and our home left to pay.

This change of mindset and lifestyle was challenging for us, but we knew that the minimal benefits of everything we were doing had too high a cost. A Cost/Benefit analysis is normally used as an economic decision-making approach. It is mainly used in government and business to see whether the benefits outweigh the costs. It usually involves conducting evaluations, taking risk and uncertainty into consideration, as well as other factors. For our purposes it will only be used to determine if the benefit of an activity you are doing outweighs the cost. I decided to sacrifice time watching TV (that was easy with no cable) and the hours I would spend on Facebook. The benefit of the time I spent on those items were minimal to what it was costing me in being happier, changing lives, and making more money to get out of debt.

---

### 💣 REFLECTION EXERCISE 6.4

What is one thing that you can sacrifice to start moving in the direction of your vision? It may be difficult, but you can do it.

_____

_____

_____

_____

_____

_____

---

I'm not a natural planner. I usually prefer to set the vision and just go, but I have realized that flying by the seat of my pants is not as effective. Whether you are a natural planner or not it's important to plan for your journey on authentic success. I'm not saying that every single step will be detailed, but you will have more direction to move in your chosen direction. Don't let planning be a chore, but make it a fun exercise and be creative in how you will get there. Remember, if you fail to plan, you plan to fail! Plan for authentic success!

---

### ✅ ACTION ITEMS:

1. Try Targeted Planning today by planning before you go to bed or in the morning. Write it down or put in your phone. Prioritize your top 3 or 4 things.
2. Write down your First Look Core Values and create 2-3 R.E.A.L. Goals for each core value.
3. Determine a person that you think will be a good Professional Accountability Partner (PrAP).

4. Conduct a personal Cost/Benefit analysis of a specific core value in your life (i.e. Finances, Friends, Career) and determine the benefits outweigh the costs or vice versa. Then make a decision to either stop or continue doing the specified activities.
5. Don't forget to share with someone else in 24 hours what you have learned from this chapter.

# Lens 3 – Targeted Planning

# CHAPTER SEVEN
# LENS 4 – INSPIRING ACTION:
# WHAT WILL I DO?

*"What we think, or what we know, or what we believe is, in the end, of little consequence. The only consequence is what we do."* — John Ruskin

*" One Dollar and a Dream "*

## Svetlana Kim

Svetlana's remarkable story begins in Leningrad, Russia. Standing in the bread line for the third day in a row, she intently listened as her neighbors talked about the impending fall of the Berlin Wall. Life as a student in what she calls a "crumbling country," offered her few possibilities. To her surprise a former classmate offered her a plane ticket to the United States, and she jumped at the opportunity.

When she arrived she only had one dollar to her name and a dream for something better. She also did not speak English, but she remembered the perseverance of her grandmother. "I often reflect on my grandmother's tales of hard times, and it gives me strength to make the very best of my own life," she said. She rose from that one dollar and is now inspiring thousands around the world with her story of perseverance, dedication, and action. Her unique experience led her to write the life-changing book, *White Pearl and I: A Memoir of a Political Refugee*. Through her action, both then and now, she is inspiring others to achieve their dreams.

## INSPIRING ACTION DEFINED

You have probably heard the phrase, "actions speak louder than words." I agree wholeheartedly with this statement. I must admit that my actions don't always line up with what I say, but I am progressing. I can't stress enough how this journey is not about perfection, but rather, progression. Don't think you have to do everything perfectly to be authentically successful. All you have to do is be honest with yourself and others, and challenge yourself to get better, do better, and act better.

*Webster's Dictionary* defines *action* as:
1. A thing done.
2. The accomplishment of a thing usually over a period of time, in stages, or with the possibility of repetition.

I simply define *action* as doing something. Inspiring ACTion is doing the right something. There are many people who are acting everyday. They act by going to work, they act by going to school, they act by playing with their children, they act by working on an internship, and so on. Not everyone has Inspiring ACTion, because this is about doing the right things. This lens is about what you actually do.

I never realized the immense importance of this step until I heard stories from participants in my presentations. I realized that there was usually a big difference between what people said and what they did. They would share their dream, what they wanted to fix in their life, or their plan to improve. However, very few were actually following through with what they said they would do. For most of my life it has been hard to follow through. There are so many competing factors. There has been school, work, family, friends, church, volunteering, and a lot of other things in my life. That is why if you use the *Clarifying Cycle of Success Model*™ it can make this process much easier. Let's learn how to ACT.

### Ellen Sirkis Katz: A Grandmother's Love

Ellen was a peculiar interview for me. When I asked Ellen if she ever struggled with making decisions and acting on her core values, she said never. While she was growing up she saw others around her making huge differences in society.

She recalled attending a funeral for a close relative and a lot of important people being at the funeral. Dignitaries in the community were not at her relative's funeral because her relative was in politics. They were not there because her relative won a Pulitzer Prize. They were not even there because her relative was a best selling author. But what she was and what she did changed the lives of people around her. Her relative sacrificed her life for others and Ellen has been determined to do the same.

Throughout Ellen's life she has given back, volunteered, and led some major initiatives within the community. One thing that really stands out to me about Ellen is her love for her grandchildren. She babysits, helps out, and does all the wonderful things grandparents do. The children are a priority for her and her actions show it. Even trying to schedule an interview with her we had to plan required planning around her time with her grandchildren. She rearranges her schedule to make sure she is there for them. Even though that was challenging to me as the interviewer it spoke volumes about what she really cares about. Ellen definitely has inspired me with her actions.

This is what Inspiring ACTion is all about. We must get to a place where our actions progressively line up with what we say is important in our lives. Are we willing to accept the consequences of never acting? Are we willing to live a life full of regrets? If you are like me, the answer is NO!!!

## THE DANGERS OF INACTION

" *The desire of the sluggard kills him, for his hands refuse to labor.*"
– Ancient Hebrew Proverb

There are many dangers that can be caused by inaction. One of the dangers is living a life that you don't love. I know so many people that never act on what is important. Every other month that I talk with them, they have a new idea, concept, or way to improve their life. The next time I talk to them, they have moved on and never fully acted on what they said they would do. For many this has led to "dead end" jobs where they are miserable. Many others are discontent with their family life, and so many others are simply just discontent with life. This is a big danger.

Are you living an unbalanced life? Are you constantly struggling with the proverbial "work/life balance" issue that so many of us face today? How are you handling the constant pressure to be more and do more in every single area in your life? The real answer to this problem is working smarter, not harder. Working on what matters more than we work on things that don't matter. Early on in my career I learned that there would always be something else to do. I had to figure out what mattered the most to my manager and the company and focus on doing those things with excellence.

## REFLECTION EXERCISE 7.1

Imagine that your life is a company and that you are the president. On a scale from 1 to 5 (with 1 being never focused and 5 being always focused), are you focusing on what matters most to your life? Do your actions communicate that your life is centered on your core values?

_____

_____

_____

_____

_____

_____

_____

Another danger of inaction is the shouldve's, wouldve's and couldve's. Because people don't act, these words become a constant theme in many people's lives. These phrases have been uttered from my mouth many times because of inaction in my past. Today is a new day. Your past is just that — your past! Don't let your lack of ACTion today lead you to saying these phrases tomorrow. Make today count. Make it matter!

In *Life Entrepreneurs*, Christopher Gergen and Gregg Vanourek discuss the cost of not acting. They share that many people pay that price of inaction just to remain in the comfort of the known. Have you not acted to remain comfortable?

I know an even worse place to be. That place is regret - regret for not even trying to go after your dreams, regret for not spending more time on what really matters in life, regret for not living the life that you were destined to live. That place is full of unhappy people and you don't want to be there. If you are there now I want you to do something for me. I want you to repeat a mantra that I use in my own life. *"You can't change what happened, but you CAN change what happens!"* We have to be careful that we don't live life through the rear view mirror, because if we do for too long we will have an accident in our future.

 ## *Guillermo Brown: A Man of ACTion*

When I met with Guillermo we were in his classroom. He is a passionate Spanish teacher at a private school. When I talked with his students I could tell that he was a special kind of teacher, one that you don't get too often. He is a teacher that really cares, and a teacher that will act on what matters for his students. Guillermo and I sat down and he shared his powerful story.

Guillermo was on his way to Venezuela to work with the Catholic Foreign Mission Society. It was originally a contract for 3 years, but he ended up staying 17 years. He saw a need and he acted on it. He stayed in Venezuela doing grass roots work in poor and marginalized communities. He was happy because he was making a difference. It was never about the money for him.

During his time in Venezuela he and his wife suffered a miscarriage; after that she had problems conceiving. Again, Guillermo acted and they decided to adopt. They moved back to Maryland for family ties. It is quite evident that he lives by Eduardo Galeano's quote, "We are what we do, to change who we are."

## WHAT PREVENTS US FROM ACTION

Several years ago I kept hearing the same question. "Where is your book?" I always felt that I was supposed to write a book, but for a long time I never did. I simply did not know where to start. I had never done it before and it seemed rather intimidating. I walked away from speaking at a university in Houston inspired to actually do write my first book. I said to myself a mantra that still holds true for me today, *"Start big, by starting small, at least just start."* This is a big problem for many, as they know what they want to do, but they just don't know where to begin. Sometimes our vision is so big that we doubt if we can really ever accomplish it. I believe in the saying that the only way to eat an elephant is one bite at a time.

I forced myself to sit down one day and just write the table of contents, to provide the structure for the book. I felt really good about it, and another day I wrote one of the chapters of the book. From there it felt like a smooth ride because the momentum was on my side. Even though writing my first book was a challenging process, as I kept writing it became easier to do. Now I am here with two books written, and I am helping others to write their books. I am helping others to start on their visions!

Let me help you. It is okay if you don't know where to start, but that is why Lens 3 - Targeted Planning is so beneficial. That lens helps us to map out how we can achieve our vision. It also challenges us to have a PrAP and a mentor. They can help us to create a starting point just to get the ball rolling and build the momentum. It reminds me of watching Strong Man Competitions. Whenever they had to pull the tractor or the big Double Decker bus the hardest part for them was getting started. It is amazing how much easier it becomes when momentum is on your side. The unfamiliarity can be paralyzing, but I can guarantee you one thing - you will never accomplish your vision if you don't try. You will never live your core values, if you do not try!

Procrastination and the fear of failure are also major reasons that people don't ACT. I believe we don't try so that we cannot fail. We keep pushing off what we are unfamiliar with because if we never do it, then we can never fail. The sad truth is that in trying not to fail, we are actually failing and don't even recognize it.

In the *Now Habit*, Neal Fiore discusses that people procrastinate. He says that the reason some people procrastinate is because if they delay beginning their work they will not be doing their best. Thus, if they fail or receive criticism it will not be a judgment on their true best effort. This was a powerful revelation for me. When I first read this it blew my mind. This has been one of the reasons I have procrastinated on much of what I have done, and I had to confront this issue in order to move forward. What about you? Have you ever felt this way?

I agree with Neil when he says procrastination is not the problem. It is merely a symptom of the real problem. There is a reason that you and I procrastinate at times. It may be because we are afraid to fail, afraid of success, unsure of ourselves, not knowing where to start, not interested in it, or any other assortment of reasons. Our greatest need is to go beyond the surface, determine what the real problem is, and address it. We need to be able to answer why we procrastinate in the first place.

## REFLECTION EXERCISE 7.2

When was the last time that you procrastinated on something that you really wanted to do? Why did you procrastinate? What can you do to move forward?

_____

_____

_____

_____

_____

_____

_____

_____

_____

_____

_____

_____

_____

This section is for all of my perfectionists who need to have everything all together before they move. I used to be a perfectionist. I had to have everything in its proper place before I acted. I would spend hours and days trying to figure out every step along the way. This is called planning paralysis. People get stuck in planning, and they are never satisfied with the plans, or when they are satisfied the time to act has already passed on that specific situation.

The FOCUS organization conducted an interview with Colin Powell. In the interview he was asked about making decisions. He replied, "The real test is not so much making decisions, as executing them." Colin Powell recognizes the need to ACT even if he doesn't have all of the information in a perfect manner.

> My own experience is that you get as much information as you can and then you pay attention to your intuition, to your informed instinct. Sometimes what my analytical mind says to me is not what I'll do. Generally you should act somewhere between P40 and P70, as I call it. Sometime after you have obtained 40% of all the information you are liable to get, start thinking in terms of making a decision. When you have about 70% of all the information, you probably ought to decide, because you may lose an opportunity in losing time.

What opportunities have you lost due to perfect planning? A way to overcome this is to acknowledge the direction that you would like to go based on your core values. Then start in that direction. I talked with a young lady at a graduation where I was the commencement speaker. She could not decide exactly what she wanted to do now that she had graduated. I informed her to take a look at her passions and strengths (Lens 1 – Reflective Thinking) and move in the direction, because if she waited to have it all planned out she may never act. I hope she took my advice. I hope you take my advice.

Sometimes people don't act because they talk too much! You may be wondering what I mean by this statement. In 2009 Peter Golwitzer, a social psychologist, conducted research on sharing your goals with others and found that those who shared their goals felt more of a sense of accomplishment without having accomplished the goal. The social acknowledgment from telling someone and them being happy about what was stated, was actually giving a similar feeling to actually accomplishing the goal.

Now you may be asking yourself if this goes against the whole concept of PrAP. It doesn't. Your PrAP does not serve as a person to just cheer you on, but this person is there to challenge you to keep moving forward. When you share your vision and goals with your PrAP it should be done in a way that has an expectation of accountability. Without accountability you may feel the positive feelings or social acknowledgement as if you already accomplished the goal. In order to stay on the track of acting, please be careful what you share and how you share your goals with others. Instead of saying, "I will finally start my own business," say, "I plan on starting my business and I need you to hold me accountable to doing it."

## ALIGNING ACTION WITH GOALS

Mentors and your PrAP can help you with to make sure that your actions align with your R.E.A.L. goals. Have you ever watched a boxing match where the person threw a lot of punches and landed very few? Those can be some of the most boring fights, because there is minimal contact, except for the constant "I am tired so I will hug you" moves. This is similar to real life if we don't ACT on our goals. Activity does not equate achievement! Just because you are busy does not mean you are getting the right things done. It is important to connect to your target.

The true test in determining if our actions align with our goals is by understanding where we spend our time. Where do you spend your time? The Bureau of Labor and Statistics conducted a survey.

The survey shows how people from the ages of 25-54 with children under 18 spend their day (see Exhibit 7.1).

**Exhibit 7.1**

## Time use on an average work day for employed persons ages 25 to 54 with children

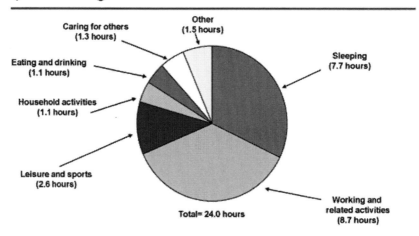

NOTE: Data include employed persons on days they worked, ages 25 to 54, who lived in households with children under 18. Data include non-holiday weekdays and are annual averages for 2009.

SOURCE: Bureau of Labor Statistics

---

### ✔ ACTION ITEMS:

1. Based on the goals that you created, ACT on one of them right away. Don't wait until you finish the book. Do it while you are reading the book.
2. Practice telling someone else your goal with the expectation of accountability, not to receive the feelings of achievement from the social acknowledgement.
3. Using Exhibit 7.1 as a guide, write out how you think you spend your time.

4. Determine if your current ACTions align with the goals and core values you have determined for yourself.
5. Don't forget to share with someone else in 24 hours what you have learned from this chapter.

# Lens 4 – Inspiring ACTion

# CHAPTER EIGHT
# LENS 5 – NAGGING PERSISTENCE:
# HOW WILL I OVERCOME?

*"Persistence is the twin sister of excellence. One is a matter of quality; the other, a matter of time."* - Marabel Morgan

---

*" 18 long years "*

## Marsheek

I t was her 12th grade year and Marsheek was looking forward to graduating. The difference was that Marsheek was not like most graduating seniors. She was the mother of 3 children. With the pressures mounting to provide for her family she decided to drop out. "That has been one of my biggest regrets, not graduating and walking across that stage," she said.

I met Marsheek at a graduation for a GED program in Baltimore, Maryland. I was there the day before to go through the dress rehearsal and I had the privilege to talk with Marsheek. She shared with me that there was a lot that she had to overcome in order to get to this point. She overcame a 22-year addiction, self-doubt, and people who said she couldn't do it. She tried several times to get her high school diploma and failed.

> I really felt frustrated that I could only get $7 per hour jobs. I wanted more for my life and for my family. I had to make a difference. I had to keep going, keep trying. I have been through so much to get here, but I am thankful I am here. Now I want to help other people who have addictions. I have to keep going!

Because she never gave up Marsheek not only received her high school diploma 18 years later, but she was able to walk across the stage. When they called her name and she walked across the stage, I saw a smile that pierced my heart. We embraced, and I felt her overwhelming joy in completing something that was so important to her. I knew that her life would be forever changed by this accomplishment. The most interesting part is that my life would be forever changed by her story. I was the one supposed to be inspiring her, and here she was inspiring me.

## NAGGING PERSISTENCE DEFINED

Marsheek is a perfect example of Lens 5 – Nagging Persistence. She fought her way through obstacle after obstacle to be able to graduate and help others. What's your story? I am sure that you have had to overcome amazing obstacles to get to where you are today. It might have been a loss of a loved one, depression, low self-esteem, not having both parents, bad relationships, or something else. The fact is that you're reading this and much of what you have experienced you have persisted through. You can probably echo the words from the Antoine Fisher movie, "It don't matter what you tried to do, you couldn't destroy me! I'm still standing! I'm still strong! And I always will be!" Every time I watch that part of the movie I get chills.

*Webster's Dictionary* defines "nagging" as, "to be a persistent source of annoyance or distraction." It defines "persistent" as:
1. Existing for a long or longer than usual time or continuously.
2. Retained beyond the usual period.

In joining the two together you get a persistence that exists for a longer than usual time. When I shared this model with others people would ask me why I picked the word "nagging." For most it has a negative connotation, but I see it differently. Some people thought about a nagging wife, others a nagging salesperson, and others nagging parents. What may have been used for negativity I think can be used for good. What if that same energy used for nagging was used to live out our vision or our core values? What if we became naggers and annoyed the heck out of mediocrity and the naysayers by existing for a longer than usual time? Nagging

Persistence is all about overcoming obstacles along the journey of authentic success, because they will come.

Did you ever play the staring game as a kid? You would look at a person and challenge him or her to not blink and see who could stare at the other person the longest. This game is the essence of Nagging Persistence, which is not giving up. Since I've always been a competitive person, I would do all I could to win. Tears would be streaming down my face because I did not want to blink. I was determined to win.

Are you determined to win in the "game" of your life? If you are, you must be willing to let the tears roll down your cheek and still continue. That's how life is, and that is why this lens is so important to the model. In your life do you feel stranded by people, experiences, or even in your job? As I stated in the introduction, revealing and achieving authentic success will not be easy. Some people may look at you like you are crazy because you are not after societal success. You may seem different, but on this journey persistence is key. Frederick Douglas said it best when he said, "Without struggle, there is no progress."

## THE VISION OBSTACLES

Have you ever felt like your vision was blocked? Well then you and I have had the same feelings. On this journey there will be other people who will be obstacles to your authentic success. In my presentations I like to call them the "haters." The haters are people who no matter what you do they just don't like you. They don't like you when you do things wrong, they don't like you when you do things right. Many times we allow the haters to be vision obstacles on our journey.

The challenge that we have is that we listen to the haters and we actually start to believe what they are saying. Because we focus so much on them, what they say becomes a reality in our lives. Let me be clear and state that just because someone does not agree with you that does not make him or her a hater. Haters are mainly defined by not having your best interests in mind. I have had several people that have challenged my visions, but there are those who are there to hate and those who are there to help.

Our focus should be on the helpers in our lives. One of my sayings is, *"We spend too much time proving our worth to others, that we are losing precious moments in being our worth!"* The helpers are the people in our lives and are supporting us toward our vision. They are the people who both challenge and encourage us, the ones who really care about us. They need more of our attention then the haters do because the haters will always be there. We need to show the helpers how much we appreciate them, and value their contributions in our lives. Sometime we do not say thank you enough to them and show them that we appreciate them. Will you start focusing more on the helpers today?

### REFLECTIVE EXERCISE 8.1
Who do you focus more on, the haters or the helpers? Why?

_____

_____

_____

_____

_____

_____

_____

_____

_____

Who is usually the biggest hater? You guessed right if you said yourself. You show that you are your own hater when you wake up the morning and say things like, "this is going to be a horrible day," or "I know that things are not going to go well today." What you have done is mentally and verbally killed your great day. You will look at the rest of the day through a lens of negativity. Once a person has this lens on it is challenging to see differently. Have you met someone like this, someone who is always negative? You walk up to them and say good morning and they say something like "what's so good about it?" That person might be looking you in the mirror and you may not even know it.

We have to deal with enemy in ourselves in order to have Nagging Persistence. We have to get out of our own way and stop sabotaging our own vision. More than likely you already know you do this, so I would encourage you to be proactive and make it one of your goals to address it. I had a serious problem with procrastination so I began to read books and go online to find ways I could improve. All it takes is a little intentionality to start seeing some changes. Here are some examples of people who operate by Lens 5 - Nagging Persistence.

 ## Wallace Arnold: Dealing with the Naysayers

Growing up in the projects was a challenge for Wallace. His father treated him like an outcast. He allowed some of these challenges to lead him to a life of dealing and using drugs. "I had the intellect, but never utilized it to go to college," he said. Down the road he finally made a decision to get his life back on track and he was offered a position as a custodian at an elementary school. He was just happy for the opportunity and that someone gave him a chance.

He did so well at that position, that he was offered a position at a university as a custodian. Again, he was so happy to have been given an opportunity that he really did well, but as things were improving he faced obstacles. He faced being surrounded with people who doubted his abilities. He faced co-workers who were not satisfied with his performance, not because he was not doing a good job, but because he was doing his job too well. He still faces challenges, but he is persevering through them.

> I still live in an area populated with drugs. With all of this I must persevere and stay focused. Sometimes I face obstacles from my own family as I am working toward my goals. Even through all of this I am so grateful for the opportunity. I am blessed to be able to work at a university when I always regretted not going. I plan on starting my college education one day soon.

### *Lawrence Richardson: A Pastor Overcoming Problems*
Lawrence grew up as a pastor's kid. He admired his dad's preaching and his mom's great wisdom. One day, he realized that he was wearing his parents' glasses of what they wanted him to be. As he came into adulthood he started to understand more about this unique view on life. Years later he married and unfortunately that relationship ended in divorce.

> She said to me, 'you will never be anything without me.' Those words cut me, stymied me, and put me in a tailspin. I looked up two years later and I was still hearing that voice and living out what she said.

This was not the last time he would hear some challenging words from someone close to him. He was attending a church, where he met his current wife. He said he knew God was birthing a ministry out of him named Living Waters, but unfortunately his pastor at the time did not see the same vision. His pastor said to him, "The vision that you have carried, you have carried too long." This time he did not pay attention to it, and he has now been the pastor of a growing and healthy church for over 12 years. "The closer we get to authentic success, the more important it becomes to know the God-given vision within. It will breed greater criticism," he said.

 *Stacie Harris: Through it all*

At the age of five Stacie realized that she loved people. That love for people would be challenged by traumatic experiences in her life. Her mother died at age 24. Her stepfather claimed that she would never be anything, but she was determined to do everything she set her heart to. She also lost her first home and lived in a transition home with her children. There were many people in her life that said she could not do well, but she is proving them wrong as a business owner, a proud mother, and an author. She possessed the will to continue through it all. Through all of the obstacles she has persisted toward her vision.

## REFLECTION EXERCISE 8.2

What is your story? What are the obstacles that you have had to overcome to get to this point in your life? Write them down and be very thankful that you have overcome them.

_____

_____

_____

_____

## THE FRAME OF FAILURE

A part of Nagging Persistence is embracing the fact that sometimes you will fail. Just because you do everything you can does not mean that you will accomplish everything you want.

My mom reminded me that I used to pull on her pants and say, "Mommy, Mommy, Mommy," until I got tired or she yelled "WHAT?" Wouldn't you call that Nagging Persistence? She wouldn't respond all of the time, but she did sometimes respond. I had to be okay with her not responding while knowing that sometimes my tactic would work. This is the same approach we must take with our vision. There are going to be some things that work beautifully and other things that will not work at all, but you must keep trying.

When I first started my speaking business I was so excited. I finally knew that this was my passion and the best part was that people were willing to bring me in to speak. I was in an MBA program and at the time the college market was my primary focus. I decided to try and speak at Freshmen Orientation. I would even offer them a discount as a current student. I met with the Assistant Director and was told no. This was devastating to me. I felt like if my own school did not want me, then no other school would want me either.

I contemplated giving up my speaking business because of the discouragement. While I was at home one day I said to myself that I am going to turn that "no" into a "yes." Instead of giving up I asked to meet with the Assistant Director and Director. I asked them why they said no, and I was informed that they usually only pick from a handful of people, and that it is usually from a certain conference. I asked them for tips on how I could grow my business and they helped me tremendously. I have now gone back and have been paid to speak for their program. I also have now spoken to tens of thousands of people. Just for the college market I have spoken to students from over 100 colleges and universities. I took that "no" that I received from them and turned it into "yes" at colleges, corporations, and churches around the country.

## TIPS FOR NAGGING PERSISTENCE

**Tip #1:** It is important to be honest with yourself, your PrAP, and your mentor concerning the obstacles you face. At times, you may feel the need to figure it our on your own, but try to rely on people to help you see the big picture. When we face challenging times we can become very shortsighted. Even though you may lose a battle, there is still a war to be won!

**Tip #2:** Learn from your mistakes along the journey. During your next time of Reflective Thinking find out how you can improve. As stated before you want to become a Progressionist, not a Perfectionist.

**Tip #3:** Talk to others who have been through something similar and are successfully on the other side. Their advice, wisdom, and experience may help you in your unique journey through the obstacles.

**Tip #4:** Have a mindset that you can do it. If you already think you cannot then you will be give out the energy and effort to match what you think. Try your hardest, and if you don't succeed try hard again. Later on you may have to shift your approach, but don't move unless you know you have given your best effort.

**Tip #5:** Recognize that some things in your life will only be temporary. You may have a job that you are doing your not currently happy with, and I understand, as I have had a couple of those. Maintain a positive attitude and learn as much as you can from the experience. Sometimes what I learned was that I needed to improve in order to truly possess happiness with certain jobs.

---

## ✔ ACTION ITEMS:

1. Take a piece of paper and draw a line down the middle. On the left side write "Haters" and on the right side write "Helpers." List the haters in your life and then list the helpers. Fold the piece of paper over so you can just see the helpers and determine to focus on them. Do one thing out of the ordinary to show them that you appreciate their help.

2. Identify an area where you have received a no, and think about how you can turn that into a yes.

3. Write out your story of overcoming obstacles and share it with someone you feel could benefit from it.

4. Don't forget to share with someone else in 24 hours what you have learned from this chapter.

# Lens 5 – Nagging Persistence

<br />

## CHAPTER NINE
## LENS 6 – APPRECIATIVE CELEBRATION:
## WHAT/WHO WILL I CELEBRATE?

*"There are exactly as many special occasions in life as we choose to celebrate."*
- Robert Brault

---

*" The Blood of a Mother "*

<br />

<br />

## Dr. Tyrone Bledsoe

D r. Bledsoe grew up in Mississippi in the midst of great racial tension, but the biggest tension in his life would come when he was 23 years old. His growth and maturity through this ordeal would help define him throughout the future.

> At the age of 23 my mother was accidentally shot in the throat. I went to the emergency room and while I was there the nurse came out and told me that my mother had died. She died on November 4, 1984. That night I had to clean her blood up with my own hands in the car and at home. I really thought that night I was going to die. I woke up in the morning and I said these words, 'I am still here.'

Being still here has encouraged him to achieve much more. Getting through that really tough time in his life challenged Dr. Bledsoe to celebrate the journey of life.

## APPRECIATIVE CELEBRATION DEFINED

How do you celebrate your life? Or do you even celebrate your life at all? If you are living right now, then I know you have much to celebrate. You have been through some things, some setbacks, some failures, but here you are. I believe our lives should reflect a lifestyle of celebration. *Webster's Dictionary* defines celebration as, "to observe a notable occasion with festivities."

As the final lens, Appreciative Celebration is sometimes a forgotten step. Authentic success is not a destination, but rather it is a journey. Therefore, there should be times of appreciation for what you gained from the journey so far. I believe that too many people go through life with so much going on that they lose sight of all the positives that are happening in and around them.

Appreciative Celebration does not have to be a big party. It could be as small as just thinking about the journey and appreciating what you can celebrate or it could be as large as a planned vacation. No matter how you choose to celebrate you should celebrate the journey.

A part of celebrating is remembering the milestones in the journey. For example, if during Targeted Planning you set a milestone of eliminating all of your credit card debt then you should celebrate after you accomplish that feat. Maybe your reward is something like going to the spa (of course not on your credit card)! The rewards can serve as great momentum as you are accomplishing your visions and goals. Without celebrating, life will pass you by and you might not enjoy what you are working so hard to accomplish.

### REFLECTION EXERCISE 9.1
How often do you celebrate the small moments in your life? Why?

_____
_____
_____
_____
_____
_____
_____
_____
_____
_____
_____
_____
_____

*Erin Hodge-Williams: The Small Moments Matter*

Erin's parents were involved in the human services field. Some holidays she remembers having disadvantaged youth join their family. This helped Erin realize her privileges in life, but it also did something more profound. It helped to fuel her passion to help others. Erin said, "I value the small moments and find the joy in simple things. I celebrate by noticing and appreciating the incremental changes." Sometimes the incremental changes are all that's seen as Erin works with youth, and she does it because she loves it.

Sometimes the changes that you will see will not always be big. It could just be doing it once, because we have already established that starting is the usually the biggest challenge. Make sure that you don't automatically move onto the next thing to accomplish without pressing "pause" in life to appreciate what you have already done.

I believe that this is one of the reasons that we do not say thank you enough to others. We expect the very next thing after they have done something wonderful. This can damage our relationships with others if we are demanding the next thing to be accomplished without letting the people in our lives know that we appreciate them!

## TIPS FOR APPRECIATIVE CELEBRATION

Appreciative Celebration also allows you to see some of your progress and what you have been able to accomplish. The following tips will help you celebrate more of the things in your life:

1. Take time to celebrate the small things that happen every day. If you made a step in the right direction take a small moment to recognize it.

2. Create a separate reward list and match the items with the goals you set. This way you will never have a shortage of ways to celebrate.

3. Choose rewards and ways to celebrate that are attractive to you. If not, then you will not be motivated by the reward. Make sure it is something you have a great interest in to help push you closer to achieving the goal.

4. Commit to only fulfilling your reward once you have completed the goal. For example, I am waiting for a big sale to occur until I purchase an iPad 2. I have been tempted to buy it now as I have the money, but that is a reward that I set up, and should abide by it. Waiting to accomplish your goals is even better with patience.

5. Share your rewards and things to celebrate with your PrAP and mentor. It is great to have public support of your accomplishments.

---

## ✔ ACTION ITEMS:

1. List three (3) people to appreciate on your journey and thank them.
2. Write down one thing that you are a thankful for and want to celebrate. Now celebrate it however you choose.
3. Don't forget to share with someone else in 24 hours what you have learned from this chapter.

# Lens 6 – Appreciative Celebration

# CHAPTER TEN
## "I" SURGERY: THE A.R.C. OF AUTHENTIC SUCCESS

*"The greatest revolution of our generation is the discovery that human beings, by changing the inner attitudes of their minds, can change the outer aspects of their lives"* – William James

## "4 months to live"

### Jordan and Danielle Rice

Jordan and Danielle were married in August of 2009; after having a challenging childhood, Danielle finally met her Prince charming. In May of 2010 Jordan and Danielle joined me for rock climbing for my birthday, as Jordan was my best friend. We all had a great time, and we looked forward for many more years to come. That is why it was surprising for me to receive a phone call from Jordan like I had never heard him before. He was crying uncontrollably and I was afraid to ask why. He said, "Justin, Danielle has cancer."

I remember being immediately paralyzed by his words, and I sunk into my chair. I was really baffled as Danielle was only 26 years old. "I felt that I was hit by a Mack truck. This was completely against the plan," Jordan said as he explained how he initially felt. The doctor shared the news with Jordan in the hallway, and they were headed in to tell Danielle. The doctor shared with Danielle that she had cancer with a prognosis of only 4 months to live. Danielle just didn't have cancer, but she had a very rare cancer. She had angiosarcoma, which only strikes about 20+ people a year. When she found out the news, she was a little shaken up about it, but the words out her mouth have resonated with me since I hear them.

Danielle said, "Well I guess it is a win-win, because either I will be in healed or I will be in heaven." What still amazes me to this day is how she could be on her deathbed and still see a win-win situation. I really thought to myself what was my excuse. What is your excuse for not seeing win-win?

Four months came and went and fortunately Danielle's cancer went into remission, but not for long. In January the cancer came back stronger than before, and over the weekend of April 1 and 2 of 2011 there were about 20 family visitors who came by the hospital. After many visits, when everyone went home she spoke very clearly to Jordan,

> Jordan I am so glad that you have all your family for your support. I am glad that you have people here for you. Justin is a really good friend for you. I am glad Justin is here for you.

They never really explicitly talked about her dying, but they had a mutual understanding. Even while Danielle was in the process of dying she was thinking about Jordan. She had only been given 4 months to live, but she was able to see their one-year anniversary, her 27th birthday party (and we did celebrate), and spend quality time with Jordan before she passed. Danielle has taught me many things through her life and suffering. She taught me how to see win-win, and she taught me how to be selfless. Her attitude was truly amazing! (To donate to clean water efforts in memory of Danielle Rice go to www.mycharitywater.org/daniellerice).

# THE A.R.C. OF SUCCESS

The A.R.C. stands for Attitude, Relationships, and Character of Success. These are three areas that are necessary to highlight when discussing authentic success. If these three areas are not addressed, the Clarifying Cycle of Success Model will only have a short-term effect.

## ATTITUDE

Attitude is essentially your mindset. It is the way you look at life. There are generally two types of attitudes. You either have a negative attitude or you have a positive attitude.

---

### REFLECTION EXERCISE 10.1
What kind of attitude do you have most of the time? Why?

_____

_____

_____

_____

_____

_____

_____

---

What kind of attitude do you prefer to be around? Most people would say positive, but I have encountered some very negative people, who are negative all the time. This impacts their outlook in life. Instead of seeing the best in situations in people they see the worse. Having a positive attitude is necessary to achieve authentic success, because you probably will not try with a negative attitude. And if you do try it won't be your best effort.

When I worked for the financial investments firm I sat in a diversity training one day, and on the screen showed the low numbers of African-Americans being promoted within HR, and on top of that there were 0% of men who had been promoted within the given time frame. I was looking at this screen as the only African-American male and wondering where I fit in within this organization. From then on I really had a horrible attitude. Because I felt I was not going to be promoted, I thought why even try. The quality of my work decreased and I was no longer as much of a team player as I was. The Power Point that I saw just reinforced what I already believed. What I did was start to look through a different lens, a more negative one. I am not saying that the numbers were wrong, because they were representative of what was occurring in the organization, but I took the wrong approach.

It almost got to the point where I was fired in order for me to wake up and see that everyone was not against me, and that I could choose which path I would take. After a few months I finally got back on track. After a few more months my department was going to recommend me for a promotion, but I left the organization before that came into fruition. Once I challenged the way I was looking at the organization and realized that I could choose my path, my whole mindset shifted. I started working harder and more productive, and I was definitely more of a team player. The wrong attitude was sending me quickly to not having a job, while the right one eventually led me to the cusp of a promotion. It really was all about my attitude and how I looked at the situation.

Sometimes I am asked the difference between having an attitude of complacency and an attitude of contentment. The two are very different. Complacency is accepting the status quo and never really trying to achieve anything more. Contentment is appreciating what you have, but still striving for more. IF you have an attitude of contentment you will appreciate more of this journey, while complacency will leave you wondering what life could have been like if you would have only tried. Danielle was content. It did not mean that she did not try all that she could to get better, but at the end of the day she was at peace.

---

### ☼ REFLECTION EXERCISE 10.2
Draw a line in the area that you feel you are in most of the time. Where are you honestly the closest to?

Complacency.......................................Contentment

---

One major point I bring up in most of my presentations is two types of people. There are the abundance people and the deficit people. The abundance people see plenty for everyone. These are people in your classes that help other students. These are employees in your company that share valuable information with others that may appear to be "competition" for a promotion. When you see abundance you usually have better relationships because you believe in investing in others.

A person seeing mainly deficit is one that sees a limited supply of something. This is a person that hoards information and does not share what could help others. He or she does not think there is enough to go around so they do all they can to keep it all in their possession. These types of people do not invest in others, as they are afraid that the competition will beat them.

The agency of CAMPUSPEAK represents me for all college audiences that I speak to, and I was their Rookie of the Year for the 2010-2011 school year. The interesting part for me is that I did all I could to share what I was doing with other speakers that wanted to know. I also attached myself to other abundance speakers that did not mind sharing freely how they were doing well. In the deficit model I would have hoarded all the information, but what probably would have happened is that I might not have gotten as much help from other speakers as well. Whichever model you choose, abundance or deficit, I believe you will receive in return at some point. On this journey it is important to see abundance and help others and also celebrate others. People who see mainly the deficit also usually see worst in life. Two of my interviewees, Tim Kassouf and Lawrence Richardson, both see themselves as eternal optimists, and therefore think that things will work to their benefit.

---

**REFLECTION EXERCISE 10.3**
Do you tend to think that things will work out to your benefit or that things are working against you? Why?

_____

_____

_____

_____

---

What attitude will you choose to have? It really is a choice more than we believe. It can be as simple as looking at the situation from a different perspective. The authentic successful people are ones with a positive attitude, an attitude of contentment, and they see things in abundance. This provides the right mental framework to achieve authentic success and to help others achieve theirs. What kind of attitude do your friends think you have, what about your co-workers or classmates?

## RELATIONSHIPS

Who you are connected is a very important piece of this authentic success journey. If you are connected to the right people they will help you along the journey, and if you are connected to the wrong people they will drag you off of the journey. Generally we know if relationships are helping us, but sometimes we need help with those on the fence.

### REFLECTION EXERCISE 10.4

List the top 10 people in your life and then indicate if they are family, friends, or professional relationships. Rank them in order of 1 (closest to you) to 10 (not as close to you)

|    | Name | (Benefit or Baggage) |
|----|------|----------------------|
| 1  |      |                      |
| 2  |      |                      |
| 3  |      |                      |
| 4  |      |                      |
| 5  |      |                      |
| 6  |      |                      |
| 7  |      |                      |
| 8  |      |                      |
| 9  |      |                      |
| 10 |      |                      |

Now who are the top 3 people you spend the most "voluntary" time with? Are they who you ranked 1-3, or are they different. If they are different why do you think they are different?

The following assessment will help you to identify where anyone in your life resides. By completing this assessment you will be able to determine if someone is a benefit, baggage, or in between. You will also be given instructions on how to move forward with them.

### Benefits or Baggage:

What are three main characteristics of a good relationship, and what are three main characteristics of a bad relationship (i.e. good being trustworthy and bad being never calls me)? A relationship is defined as all types (family, friends, and significant others). List your responses below.

Good Relationships:
1.
2.
3.

Bad Relationships:
1.
2.
3.

Next, pick (3) of your current closest relationships (do not base who you pick on what you listed above).

Your (3) Current Closest Relationships:

| |
|---|
| Relationship 1: |
| Relationship 2: |
| Relationship 3: |

Based on the relationships you chose above, rate each of the (3) relationships from 1 to 5 (with 1 being never do this and 5 being always do this). Do this first on the (3) good relationship characteristics and then do this for the (3) bad relationships characteristics. (See Appendix C for an example).

| **GOOD** | 1 | 2 | 3 | Sub Total |
|---|---|---|---|---|
| Relationship 1: | | | | |
| Relationship 2: | | | | |
| Relationship 3: | | | | |

| **BAD:** | 1 | 2 | 3 | Sub Total |
|---|---|---|---|---|
| Relationship 1: | | | | |
| Relationship 2: | | | | |
| Relationship 3: | | | | |

| **OVERALL** | **Good Score** | **- (minus)** | **Bad Score** | **Total Score** |
|---|---|---|---|---|
| Relationship 1: | | | | |
| Relationship 2: | | | | |
| Relationship 3: | | | | |

| Rating Scale | Benefit, Baggage, or Both | 3 C's (Celebrate, Communicate, and Cut-off) |
|:---:|:---:|:---:|
| 9 to 12 | Great Benefit | Celebrate |
| 5 to 8 | Benefit | Celebrate and Communicate |
| -4 to 4 | Benefit/Baggage | Communicate |
| -8 to -5 | Baggage | Consider Cut-off |
| -12 to -9 | Great Baggage | Immediately Cut-off |

The Three C's:

♦ **Celebrate:** For either the great benefit or benefit relationships in you life you want to celebrate them. You want to let them know how much they mean to you. Do something special to show them that they are celebrated in your life. After all they are a benefit to your life.

♦ **Communicate:** For the benefit and benefits/baggage relationships you want to share with them what you like about your relationship as well as share with them ways that you think it can be improved. Do not only communicate your expectations to them, but also ask acknowledge there may be ways for you to improve as well.

♦ **Cut-off:** For the baggage and great baggage relationships these are people that you need to let go from your life, because they appear to holding you down greatly. What I mean by let go may just mean you do not spend as much time with them, while you focus on those who are either on the fence or already benefits to you. Seriously consider cutting off the baggage relationships, but immediately cut-off the great baggage relationships because it is evident they are not helping you at all.

In *Untie the Knots that Tie Up Your Life*, Ty Howard shares a similar concept when he states, "A 'toxic' relationship is a relationship where the emotions and unpleasant conditions of that relationship have escalated to continuous, undesirable situations. I cannot stress enough how important it is to have quality relationships on your journey. These people will help push you even closer toward authentic success.

*The 80/20 Rule:*
Normally the 80/20 rule is used to describe in business or an organization how 80% of the people account for 20% of the profit, where the remaining 20% of the people account for 80% of the profits. I have adapted to this rule to apply it to relationships as I have seen similarities.

In 2009, I faced some major decisions in my life; one of them was how I would move forward with some of the relationships in my life. I was like most people. I spent 20% of my time, energy, and efforts on the 20% of people who were closest to me. I spent 80% of my remaining time on the remaining 80% of people. I discovered that this was not beneficial to my growth and development. Essentially I was trying to be friends with everyone.

I decided to apply the 80/20 rule to my relationships and I began to spend 80% of my time, energy, and effort on the 20% of the people who were closest to me and the remaining 20% of my time, energy, and effort on the remaining 80% of people. This small adjustment in my life has had a major impact. Instead of focusing on the quantity of "friends" I had, I focused on the quality of friends. The top 20% are the people that understand me, that challenge me because they care about me, and they allow me to "wear my glasses" with them. I am a very high-energy person and over the years I have realized that not everyone can accept my energy so I end up turning it down for some people. With my 20% I do not have to do that. I can be authentic Justin.

I am able to give a lot more, invest in, and cultivate my short list of friends in my life. I do not ignore or shun the remaining 80%, but I also don't spend a lot of time there. This change has led to increased happiness, better relationships, and it has helped me to develop a community of people that I care about and that also care about me.

---

### 🔴 REFLECTION EXERCISE 10.5

Can you identify with my past experience? Who are you really giving your effort, initiative, time and everything to? Focus on your top 20% and making sure that they are quality and they are the people you are spending more time with. What can you do to focus more on the top 20% of people in your life?

---

Along this journey I have discovered that there are six types of people in our lives. It is what I call the 6 C's of Relationships.

♦ **Cowards:** These are the type of people who like to talk about you, but not to you. They might smile in your face, but they are calling you names and talking negatively about you to others. They don't have your best interests at heart.

♦ **Complainers:** These are the type of people who always have something negative to say about what you are doing. The difference is that they will at least tell you to your face. The complainers in our lives can be very draining.

♦ **Crowd:** These are the indifferent people. You may have surface level conversations with them, but you are not really invested in their lives and they are not really invested in your life. I classify these types of people by stating that if they were to move away, it really would not have much of an impact on you.

♦ **Comrades:** These are the people that your are invested in. You may talk to them 1-2 times a week and they have an impact on your life. You may spend time with them, and you sincerely care about their well-being. You like spending time with this group of people.

♦ **Champions:** These are the best friend type of people. You can count on them to be there through both the good times and the bad times. You usually only get 1-3 of these people in a lifetime as they are rare in relationships. You may talk to them, every day or every other day. They will encourage you, challenge you, tell you when you are wrong, and celebrate you when you have achieved.

♦ **Coaches:** These people are the true mentors in your life that help along the journey. They share their wisdom and knowledge with you to help you avoid mistakes and pitfalls. They care about your overall direction in life.

You will want to ignore the cowards, challenge the complainers to stop being so negative, enjoy the crowd, encourage the comrades, treasure the champions, and celebrate the coaches. As you view the people around you, what category do they fall in? What category do you fall in with others?

The relationships in our lives are integral, therefore we should be very intentional. I used to just let things flow and try to see where things would pan out, but I lost some really good friends along the way doing that. I also kept some really bad relationships around a lot longer than they should have been. Make having quality relationships a priority in your life or else you might be carrying around unnecessary dead weight.

# CHARACTER

 *Corey Ciocchetti: Character that matters.*

Corey sat in his high school counselor's office and he was baffled by what he heard. His counselor told him that college wasn't for him. Corey disregarded that message on went on to be a "successful" lawyer, but overtime he realized he was not happy. Six months into his career as a lawyer he was asleep on the office floor many nights, because he was working so many hours. He believed that hard work would yield benefits, but questioned if this was what he really wanted to do. "In the course of this sacrifice, I was taking years off of my life," he said.

Corey made that shift and started his own sports company and he was approached to become an Ethics professor. He still teaches and is passionate about shaping and inspiring the new generation of students. Throughout his classes and presentations he shares that character is a must and it really is about what you do when no one is watching that matters.

*Character Defined*

What I have realized is that if you ask ten different people what character is, you will receive ten different responses. I agree with Corey that character is all about what you do when no one is watching. I call this the Private Look, because if we could really tell who a person is if we could observe them in private, without them knowing we are watching. It is about the essence of your heart and the balance of your life. It is integrity with your self and others. Without a strong character the journey of authentic success will be short-lived.

---

**🔴 REFLECTION EXERCISE 10.6**

Rate the current level of your character from 1 to 5 (with 1 being the lowest and 5 being the highest). Why did you rate yourself this way? What can you do to improve your character?

_____

_____

_____

_____

---

Early on in my career I had a manager who was very intimidating. He intimidated you into doing what he wanted you to do. Being so young in my career I allowed the intimidation to affect my character. I said, "allowed" because it is always a choice.

My manager was out of the office for some time, and I took a vacation day. While I was on vacation he asked me what I was doing and I lied and said I was at work. He knew that I was not at work because he called there asking for me.

I felt so embarrassed, but even more I felt so bad inside. I am not a person who believes in lying, but I caved under pressure. Because of my low character at that moment, he never looked at me the same. No matter what I said he questioned whether I was lying or telling the truth. Our relationship was never repaired from that one lie, and to this day I regret it.

What about you? Have there been moments in your past or maybe even in your present that you are not proud of, that you wish you could take back, that you get this sickening feeling when you think about it. That is why there is such a need for great character on this journey. Without it, it can throw you off the journey of authentic success at a moment's notice.

I also believe that there is character to authentic success. This is a hard thing to define, but I believe that what you do should not hurt the overall good of mankind. I have kept this very vague on purpose, because this does not mean that you have to work for a no-profit, or be a counselor, or work in the human services field. It does mean that what you do, to the best of your ability, should not hurt the overall good of mankind.

Many people can use the model I created, and it can be for great purposes. However, the character of success should not be used to maliciously hate others. I am not saying you have to disagree with everything everyone else believes, but you should not cause harm to others with your "success."

---

### ✔ ACTION ITEMS:

---

1. Do something special to say thank you to the great relationships in your life. Show them how much you appreciate them. Write down whom you will appreciate, how you will appreciate them, and when you will do it by.

2. Determine how you will cut-off the excess weight in your life. Do not linger on this one, because I know many never got up the courage and they are still in damaging relationships.

3. Do just one thing to improve your character. It is that important to your authentic success, and if you need to right a wrong, apologize to someone, or ask for forgiveness; take the opportunity to do it.

4. Determine whether you a Champion or a Coach to someone, and if you are then find out how you can improve. Conduct the Plus/Delta analysis we learned about in Chapter 2.

5. Don't forget to share with someone else in 24 hours what you have learned from this chapter.

# CHAPTER ELEVEN

# MY GLASSES REVEALED: THE ADJUSTMENT PERIOD

*"The real voyage of discovery consists not in seeking new lands, but seeing with new eyes."* – Marcel Proust

---

## *"The Face in the Water"*

The Journey of Erin the Eagle continued:

*(From beginning of the book - pg. 1)*

A t this point, Erin was very tired and she had a headache from wearing three different pairs of glasses. She found a lake and decided to rest. After so much frustration, she saw an animal in the water that looked foreign to her, one that she thought she recognized but looked much different than any animal she had ever seen. She noticed the sun touching the water and she thought to her self, *it's worth a try*. Erin said to this strange animal, "I have been to Rob the Rabbit, Sylvester the Snake, and Olivia the Owl and have not found my glasses. I am faster, more persuasive, and wiser, but I still cannot see clearly. Do you know where my glasses are?"

The animal looked right into Erin's eyes and began to speak. "I know exactly where your glasses are. Let me share a secret with you." Erin, a little perplexed, decided to engage in this conversation. As the animal spoke Erin's eyes became bigger and bigger and bigger. The animal told Erin to take off the glasses she had acquired from Rob the Rabbit, Sylvester the Snake, and Olivia the Owl. Erin took them off and the strange animal asked Erin, "Why did you listen to the voice in the dream that said you needed glasses? You could see clearly before. Erin, you don't need the glasses given to you. It is your natural look, your authentic look that you need."

At that very moment Erin began to see clearly again and noticed that this strange animal was not so strange, but rather it was her own reflection in the lake. Erin immediately flew off to find Rob the Rabbit, Sylvester the Snake, Olivia the Owl and any others who would come back to the lake. She desired to help them also see their "strange animal" in the water and hear from a reflection that would change the course of their lives.

## WHERE ARE YOUR GLASSES

Will you look at the lake in your life? Will you engage in conversation with the "strange creature" looking back at you? Why wait another moment to decide to live your unique prescription on life, which was designed just for you! The lake is waiting for you!

Your glasses are just like Erin the Eagle's. They are non-existent. Your true glasses are your authentic look at life with your core values as a filter. Life hits you and is focused through the 6 Basic Lenses and filtered through your core values.

We have been conditioned for many years to believe that we have to wear the glasses of societal success to be somebody. Whether you have societal success or not doesn't determine your success. What determines your success is by making sure that your actions are in line with your core values.

My wife and I went to a marriage conference. We were actually doing really well in our marriage, but we believe in the philosophy that you don't have to wait until something is wrong to start making it better. We received a lot of great information, but there were a couple of key moments that stood out to me. One of the speakers was a former professor. He and his wife spoke about that process. After the conference was over I went up to him and told them of my desire to get my PhD in business in the future. I shared with them that I had recently gone to a PhD preparation conference and was told that if I wanted to be the best it would take 60-80 hours a week. I felt that would put a strain on my marriage. I told him that I heard horror stories of many divorces and strained marriages through the PhD process, and that I was not willing to sacrifice my marriage for it.

He looked at me with a glimmer in his eyes and asked me one simple question. He said, "Justin, what do you call a med student who graduates at the bottom of their class?" I said that I was not sure. His smile grew and he said, "a doctor." At that moment thousands of light bulbs were going off in my head. I understood what his question's intent was, and even more so what the answer represented. Even though the med student graduated at the bottom of his class, he still graduated and he is still a doctor. He may not have won all the awards, or received an abundance of grant money, but he still graduated.

I believe in excellence and giving it your all, but I don't believe in sacrificing what is very important to me for my PhD. It was at that moment that I gave up desiring to be the best in my career. I have always wanted to be the best in sports, school, and my career. I saw that example from my dad as he worked for the United Nations. He is a very accomplished man and is at the top in his field, but he also comes home late in the evening and even works on some weekends. I admire my dad's desire to do well, but my desire is to spend more time with my family. Don't get the wrong idea. My dad loves his wife and his three sons. I just don't desire his glasses.

I will be an excellent speaker, author and professor, but I am kay with never being the best in those areas. I will strive to be the best Christian, husband, and father I can be. I have realized that there will probably always be someone willing to sacrifice his or her family, their faith, or anything else in order to achieve societal success. But I will do everything I can to make sure that I don't do the same thing. I encourage you to make sure that you don't sacrifice your main core values for the pursuit of societal success.

There was another speaker at the conference who mentioned how he has never pressured his children to get all A's. This seemed strange to me He said that he always encouraged his children to do well in school, but he never wanted to create an environment where they are always studying. He wanted to spend time with them as a family. He said that all of his children have done well in school, but more importantly they laughed, played, and grew together as a family. This was a great example of a person who had found his or her glasses.

## A CHANGING PERSPECTIVE

There are many things in this book that challenge us to change our perspectives. We are challenged in the areas of relationships, goals, attitude, and most importantly how we define success.

## REFLECTION EXERCISE 11.1

You may have done this activity before. Connect all the dots below, but your pencil (use a pencil just in case you need to erase some of the line) cannot leave the paper. Your pencil cannot start at a new dot once you have started, and you can only use four straight lines. It must be a continuous flow once you start.

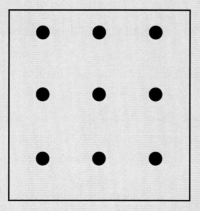

I hope that you were able to do it. If not, please go to Appendix C to see the answer before reading any further.

This is just how we treat life. I remember my first time doing this activity I was locked into the box as well. I could not figure it out either. That is what we do once we have a certain mindset. We get locked into something being a certain way and it almost feels impossible to see it differently, but this is what we must do or we might waste our lives on things that will not matter in the end. We have to allow our minds to be renewed and not conformed to the patterns of this world. In one of CS Lewis' books, he has been known to say

We all want progress. But progress means getting nearer to the places where you want to be. And if you have taken a wrong turning, then to go forward does not get you nearer. If you are on the wrong road, progress means doing an about-turn and walking back to the right road; and in that case the man who turns back soonest is the most progressive man.

Don't be a victim of the popularity mindset. The popularity mindset has left many souls desiring to be able to go back and live their core values. In order to not be a victim you have to take responsibility. You have to believe that you have the power of choice. You can choose what you will do, what your response will be, who your friends are, and many other things. If we don't choose wisely it is our fault.

We also have to challenge our limiting beliefs. Limiting beliefs are things that we believe are absolute, like someone saying he or she will never finish high school, or college, or his or her professional degree. This is also seen when people put unfair limits on their life based on what they see around them. If people who hate their job but go everyday surround you, you may feel that is what your life is going to look like. I dare you to dream and think outside the box. I would have never imagined I would be where I am today as an entrepreneur and author, but I challenged what I saw around me and didn't settle for less then I thought I was worth. You are worth more than settling for a life lived poorly, and I am not talking about monetarily. I am talking about the essence of your life.

Cheryl Gilman says in her book *Doing the Work You Love* that we will always be right. We can always find reasons why we cannot do the work we love. I want to say that we will always find reasons why we cannot reveal and achieve authentic success. Do not find excuses that you cannot be on the journey, but find reasons that you should.

## AUTHENTIC SUCCESS AND YOUR CAREER

### *Nona Carroll: My family is Worth Fighting For.*

When Nona first started working as a Trainer/Consultant for a financial investments firm she spent a lot of time working at home. She was developing training programs, but she felt like she was living to work. She became obsessed with doing work. "It was 9 at night and I was checking email," Nona said. "I even started doing work on the weekend. It started to stress me out, and I didn't want my kids to grow up without me." A big catalyst occurred when her husband started noticing she was doing a lot of work at home and he approached her about it.

Nona soon realized that something had to change. She wanted to do more with her family like helping her kids with their homework and just being there for them. She sat down with her manager and expressed her need for balance. She let him know that if he allowed her to come in early and leave at 4:00pm every day she would be sure to get all of her work done, and when she was at work she would be working really hard. She just wanted to make sure that when it was time to go home that she would be able to go home and not feel like she had to check her Blackberry. She said that the conversation was very important, because if she had started leaving at 4pm he would have looked at her differently.

Nona's manager was on board and she came in early at left at 4:00pm most days. She still faced negative perceptions from others about her truncated schedule, but as long as she got her work done and she was on the same page she knew that she was okay. Nona stated, "What happens at home is what life is all about. You can't worry about it. You need to leave work at work."

Nona did well in her role and was even promoted to a diversity role within the company. The funny thing is that she actually was paid more to do what she loved to do. Nona has societal success, but she did not pursue it. She pursued her core values and the things came to her.

Are you doing work that is meaningful? Are you happy to go to work each day? Are you in a field that you love and are passionate about? There really is no legitimate reason not to be, but it might take some adjustments. I took a pay cut and a loss of power when I went into the world of training and development, but it has paid off. Much of what I learned then I am able to incorporate into my business. According to a 2008 report by the Conference Board more than half of all Americans are unhappy with their job. I created a tool to help you diagnose where you are and where you should be. It is called the Finding Your Glasses Career Quadrant.

**Exhibit 11.1**

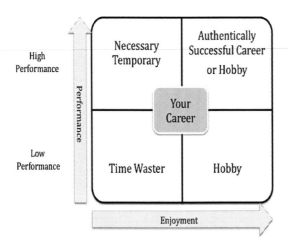

Much of career fulfillment is built on passion but also strengths. How would you define authentic strength? Most people define it by saying it is something that someone does well. However, there are many people who do things well, but hate what they do, so does that not make it an authentic strength? An authentic strength is both something that you do well and something that you gain enjoyment from doing.

Based on your current career, where are you in the quadrant? Are you at a Time Waster, because if so you need to start looking for another job right now. You probably already know that. Are you at a Necessary Temporary where you are doing well, but you just aren't that fulfilled. Sometimes these are necessary to learn a new industry or to take care of your family, but please remember it is only supposed to be necessary. Many people stay in the Necessary Temporary Quadrant for the duration of their life. Are you in the Hobby Quadrant where you really like doing something, but cannot really do it that well? I like to run, but I will more than likely never get paid to do it. I am realistic about my skill sets and running is not one of them. However I am very intentional about my hobby. If you are in the Authentically Successful Career Quadrant then you probably love your job!

A person who I used to work with chose not to do music full-time because he never wanted it to be about the money. He just wanted to do it because he loved it. He chose to work at a job that he likes, but he is very intentional about his hobby.

Do all you can to at least get to a point where you can choose either Authentically Successful Career or Hobby.

Here are a few tips on your journey for an authentically successful career:

1. Don't define yourself by what you do, but define yourself by who you are.

2.  Ask yourself the following questions:
    a.  What do I love to do?
    b.  When I die I want people to say...?
    c.  If I knew that failure was not an option,  I would...?
    d.  The career I have  always dreamed about doing is...?
    e.  What would I do for free, or what  am I  doing for free?

---

### ✔ ACTION ITEMS:

1.  How can you begin looking at success differently?
2.  Determine if it is time for you to switch careers by using the Finding Your Glasses Career Quadrant.
3.  Don't forget to share with someone else in 24 hours what you have learned from this chapter.

# CHAPTER TWELVE

# THE CONTACT LENS: SEEING BEYOND SELF

*"No person has the right to come into this world and go out of it without leaving behind them legitimate distinct reason for having passed through it."*
- Corey Ciochetti

---

## *" A Factory and a Mother's Love"*

### *Valerie Jones, my mother*

My mother raised me in Grand Rapids, Michigan. I spent about 14 years of my first 18 years of life there. During my junior year, my mother received a job in Nebraska. I stayed with one of my friends and his family. While she was away I started competing in speaking competitions on a local level. I began to win the local competitions. I then competed in regional and national oratory competitions, and my mom knew that the family I was staying with would not be able to travel with me. She moved back from her job and worked at a factory over the summer to support us. She provided a great example of being selfless.

## THE CONTACT LENS DEFINED

This lens is all about serving others. Who do you have contact with in order to serve them? Authentic Success should never just stop with it being about us. It should also be about helping other people achieve their vision. It should be about serving someone else as well.

How will you use your authentic success to show that it is much bigger than you? One of the things that I say based on an original Jim Rohn quote is, "If you work hard at your job, you can make a living. If you work hard on yourself you can make a life. If you work hard on others, you can make a difference!" I challenge you to do something for someone else after reading this book. Once Erin the Eagle found her glasses she immediately went to find the other animals. Will you do the same?

Many of the people I interviewed for the book are helping other people directly with their businesses or non-profits. Will you challenge yourself to see beyond the reflection in the water and see the rest of the forest that needs you? The following are doing this very thing. Check them out if you can.

1. Jim McCorkell, President and CEO of Admissions Possible.
2. Suzanne Mekechnie Klahir, President-CEO, BUILD Program.
3. Andrews Kwabena Nyantakyi, Chief Executive Officer of Agape Village of Hope International (Ghana).

## YOUR CHALLENGE

The rest of this chapter is to be written by you with what you do. Use the following pages to begin to note what you are doing to make a difference and how you are helping others. Will your pages be empty or will they be full with dates, times, and descriptions of how you have helped others?

---

## ✔ ACTION ITEMS:

---

1. Do something for someone else!
2. Don't forget to share with someone else in 24 hours what you have learned from this chapter.

What I will do:

---------------------------------------------------------

---------------------------------------------------------

---------------------------------------------------------

---------------------------------------------------------

---------------------------------------------------------

---------------------------------------------------------

---------------------------------------------------------

---------------------------------------------------------

---------------------------------------------------------

---------------------------------------------------------

---------------------------------------------------------

---------------------------------------------------------

---------------------------------------------------------

---------------------------------------------------------

---------------------------------------------------------

---------------------------------------------------------

---------------------------------------------------------

---------------------------------------------------------

# The Contact Lens

---

# Finding Your Glasses

_____

_____

_____

_____

_____

_____

_____

_____

_____

_____

_____

_____

_____

_____

_____

_____

_____

_____

_____

_____

_____

_____

_____

_____

_____

# Finding Your Glasses

-----------------------------------------------------------

-----------------------------------------------------------

-----------------------------------------------------------

-----------------------------------------------------------

-----------------------------------------------------------

-----------------------------------------------------------

-----------------------------------------------------------

-----------------------------------------------------------

-----------------------------------------------------------

-----------------------------------------------------------

-----------------------------------------------------------

-----------------------------------------------------------

-----------------------------------------------------------

-----------------------------------------------------------

-----------------------------------------------------------

-----------------------------------------------------------

-----------------------------------------------------------

-----------------------------------------------------------

-----------------------------------------------------------

-----------------------------------------------------------

-----------------------------------------------------------

-----------------------------------------------------------

# The Contact Lens

_____

_____

_____

_____

_____

_____

_____

_____

_____

_____

_____

_____

_____

_____

_____

_____

_____

_____

_____

_____

_____

_____

_____

# Finding Your Glasses

_____

_____

_____

_____

_____

_____

_____

_____

_____

_____

_____

_____

_____

_____

_____

_____

_____

_____

_____

_____

_____

_____

_____

_____

# The Contact Lens

# APPENDIX A

- (Change Management) *ADKAR: How to Implement Successful Change in Our Personal lives and Professional Careers* by Jeffrey Hiatt
- (Change Management) *Who Moved my Cheese* by Spencer Johnson
- (Business Improvement) *Good to Great* by Jim Collins
- (Personal Improvement) *Real Rabbits: Chasing a n Authentic Life* by Corey Ciocchetti
- (Personal Improvement) *Unleashing Your God-Given Dreams* by Steve Munsey
- (Personal Improvement) *The Road Less Traveled* by M. Scott Peck, M.D
- (Personal Improvement) *Success is not an Accident* by Tommy Newberry
- (Personal Improvement) *Creating Your Best Life* by Caroline Adams Miller and Dr. Michael Frisch
- (Personal Improvement) *Life Entrepreneurs: Ordinary People Creating Extraordinary Lives* by Christopher Gergen and Gregg Vanourek
- (Personal Improvement) *Now, Discover your Strengths* by Marcus Buckingham
- (Personal Improvement) *See You at the Top* by Zig Ziglar
- (Personal Improvement) *The Dream Giver* by Bruce Wilkinson
- (Personal Improvement) *The Focus Filled Life* by Ed Turose
- (Personal Improvement) *Release Your Brilliance: 4 Steps to Transforming Your Life and Revealing your Genius to the World* by Simon T. Bailey
- (Personal Improvement) *Inspiration for LIFE: Dream Bigger, Do More, Live Fuller!* by Justin Jones-Fosu
- (Personal Improvement) *The Last Lecture* by Randy Pausch
- (Planning／Goals) *Time Management* by Marc Mancini
- (Planning／Goals) *Goals!* By Brian Tracy
- (Planning／Goals) *Eat That Frog* by Brian Tracy

# APPENDIX B

10% of all profits will be donated to charity or other non-profit organizations that are helping people around this world:

To donate toward clean water efforts in memory of Danielle Rice please go to the website below and donate to the campaign listed. Thank you for being a part of the solution!

# www.mycharitywater.org/daniellerice

# APPENDIX C

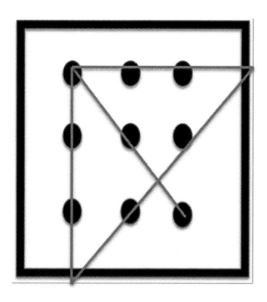

Justin Jones-Fosu

To Contact Justin or to invite Justin to Speak:

www.justininspires.com

THANKY YOU and enjoy the journey!

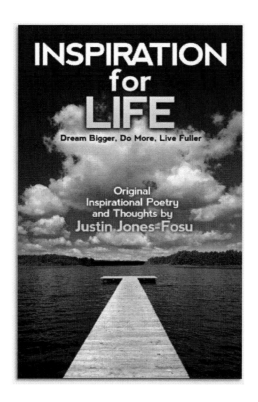

**\*Receive 10% off Justin's first book (Inspiration for Life: Dream Bigger, Do more, Live Fuller) with the code "FYG".**
**To purchase go to www.justininspires.com**